BERKELEY:
An Introduction

Jonathan Dancy

Basil Blackwell

Copyright © Jonathan Dancy, 1987

First published 1987

Basil Blackwell Ltd
108 Cowley Road, Oxford OX4 1JF, UK

Basil Blackwell Inc.
432 Park Avenue South, Suite 1503,
New York, NY 10016, USA

It is Blackwell policy to use acid-free paper for all
hardbacks. However, in order to keep down the
price of this textbook we have used a part-mechanical
paper for both hardback and paperback editions.

British Library Cataloging in Publication Data

Dancy, Jonathan
Berkeley: an introduction.
1. Berkeley, George
I. Title
192   B1348

ISBN 0-631-14525-7
ISBN 0-631-15509-0Pbk

Library of Congress Cataloging in Publication Data

Dancy, Jonathan.
Berkeley, an introduction.

Bibliography: p.
1. Berkeley, George, 1685–1753. I. Title.
B1348.D36 1987   192   86-31038
ISBN 0-631-14525-7
ISBN 0-631-15509-0 (pbk.)

Typeset by Alan Sutton Publishing, Gloucester
Printed in Great Britain.

for my mother and father

Contents

Introduction

This book is intended to provide an introduction to the main doctrines of Berkeley's *Principles of Human Knowledge* and *Three Dialogues Between Hylas and Philonous*, the works most commonly read by students and which indeed bring most readers to Berkeley. It is an expansion of a course of lectures which I have been giving at the University of Keele for a number of years, though anyone who heard an early version of them will find that they have changed considerably in the process. I expect my readers to have read their Berkeley first. I doubt very much whether what I have to say will be comprehensible otherwise, and would in many ways prefer that it should not be.

The book is intended to be largely intelligible to first year philosophy students in the UK, and therefore to persistent amateurs. No knowledge whatever of philosophy is assumed, though I do not flatter myself that I have made everything both clear and simple. Despite its main intended readership, however, I hope that there is enough in it to render it interesting to more advanced students; and there may even be some thoughts here that will interest Berkeley scholars. As befits its status as an introduction, the text is largely free of references to articles and commentaries, for the sake of simplicity. But there is a restricted bibliography at the end, in the form of suggestions for further reading chapter by chapter.

It goes almost without saying that my views about Berkeley owe an enormous amount to previous writers; and I regret that A. C. Grayling's book on Berkeley appeared too late for me to take as much account of it as I would have liked, particularly in view of the fact that I find his account of Berkeley by far the closest to my own. But I have avoided revealing the extent of my indebtedness item by item as we go along, in an attempt to keep the discussion flowing. The final chapter does at least contain some remarks about the points on which I differ most from my predecessors. It may fairly be taken that on other points the views expressed here are reasonably standard and therefore potentially derivative; though this is no guarantee at all that they are true, and no excuse for my adopting and repeating them if they are not.

My general idea when writing was to render Berkeley's doctrines as I see them accessible and interesting to comparatively inexperienced readers, and in particular to show the sorts of ways in which they contribute to contemporary (1980s) philosophical thought. A student should, after reading this book, be in a position to understand and assess the frequent references to Berkeley in contemporary writing. I have not set out to write a scholarly book about Berkeley and the tradition in which he wrote; as will be clear, I am not equipped to do so.

References are given to the *Principles* by paragraph, as P. 33 (e.g.) or PI. 10 for the Introduction to the *Principles*: and to the *Three Dialogues* by page numbers in the standard Luce and Jessop edition of Berkeley's complete works (London: Nelson 1948). The *Principles* and the *Three Dialogues* are, with other useful works by Berkeley, to be found in M. R. Ayers (ed.) *George Berkeley: Philosophical Works* (London: Dent 1975) in the margins of which the Luce and Jessop page numbers for the *Three Dialogues* are helpfully printed. Without this, reference to the *Three Dialogues* becomes almost impossible.

This is my opportunity to express my gratitude to students, colleagues and friends who have given me much helpful advice, some of which I have been rash enough to reject: John Bowen, David McNaughton, Ruth Miller, Ufuoma Ofogba, John Rogers and Jim Urmson. I owe thanks to all these, and also to David Bakhurst, Nick Dent and Bob Hargrave, who read the whole book in its penultimate version, and have made it much better than it would otherwise have been. More importantly, I owe thanks to my wife Sarah for giving me room to write in.

1

The Background

G. E. Moore once said that there are two kinds of philosophers. First there are those who can work as if in a vacuum; they are entirely taken up with philosophical problems, and their interest in them is not dependent upon what other philosophers have said about them. Second, there are those whose interest is primarily aroused by what others have said; these would happily leave the subject alone, were it not for the stupid, extraordinary or outrageous views expressed by others.

The best and perhaps the only way to come to understand the central strands of Berkeley's thought is to approach it from a (very slight) knowledge of his predecessor, John Locke. It was Locke's philosophy as much as anything that aroused his philosophical fire, though Locke appears really as a representative of a group whose leader was Newton. Berkeley had great respect for the scientific achievements of this group, but felt that those achievements had been unfortunately associated with an unacceptable philosophy. This philosophy had been most clearly expressed by Locke, who was all the same only putting into order ideas which had been expressed by the others; he speaks of himself as an underlabourer,[1] employed in clearing the ground for the work of such as Boyle, Sydenham and Huygens, as well as of Newton. This means that although there are in fact more references to Newton than to Locke in Berkeley's writings, the simplest way in for us is still through Locke.

Luckily, the essence of Locke's views can be expressed for our purposes quite briefly; so we do not have to spend a long time on one thinker in order to understand the second. There are two critical questions to which we need to understand Locke's answers. First, what is the world like? Second, how can we come to know anything about it?

Locke held that the macroscopic objects that make up the material

---

[1] This is in the Epistle to the Reader, which acts as a foreword to his *Essay Concerning Human Understanding*, edited in 2 vols. by John Yolton (London: Dent, Everyman's Library 1961), p. xxxv. In further references to and quotations from this work it will be referred to as the *Essay*.

world consist basically of atoms, molecules or corpuscles, microscopic portions of matter, held in suspension somehow (in a way of which we cannot conceive). These molecular corpuscles have only a rather limited range of properties; they have a size and a shape, they are solid (i.e. they take up space) and they can move from place to place. They have no texture or composition, because *ex hypothesi* they are the smallest sort of thing there can be. And they have no colour or temperature either.

This austere view of the microscopic is repeated when we turn to the macroscopic. Large-scale physical objects such as mice, elephants, trees and ice have shape, size, solidity and mobility, but have no colour or temperature. The only difference is that they do have a texture or composition, since they consist of molecules held together in some sort of structure.

This remark is not quite right; it needs qualification, which we can give by focusing on the notion of colour. Locke wants to say at the end of the day that material objects do have colour in a sense, though perhaps not the sense we originally thought. But to provide the needed qualification we have first to mention Locke's views about perception or, in the case of colours, sight. What is it like to see a material object? Somehow the object has an effect on us when we open our eyes in suitable light, and the only sort of effect Locke could conceive of was mechanical, as instanced classically by the workings of a clock. Inside a clock various bits are moving about pushing other bits, which have to move unless something is holding them. Locke conceived of all physical motion and change on this model. Physical events are the effects of the mechanical operations of large and/or small lumps of matter. So the same must be true for perception, which is after all in some degree a physical process. If the object we see has an effect on us, this must be because particles of some sort are travelling from it and striking our eyes. But this mechanical operation is not all there is to seeing. When we see an object, the object appears to us or looks to us to be in a certain way, and our story has not yet mentioned this important side of things. Locke conceived of the event of an object's looking to us in a certain way as the creation of a certain *idea* in our minds, a visual/perceptual idea which if we are lucky is caused by a suitable external object. And with this notion of the idea caused in the mind by an external object we can now give Locke's full account of what it is to *see* an object. We see an object when we have an idea in our minds which is caused by a suitable object. So if I have a tree-like idea caused by a suitably shaped tree, I am seeing the tree. Of course all ideas are caused by something; it is only the ones caused by suitable external objects which are visual/perceptual ideas. And an object counts as suitable if it is *like* the idea it causes – if it resembles it sufficiently.

This notion of resemblance is crucial here, for otherwise the account would hold that we see anything which causes the ideas we are currently having. And this would clearly be wrong. The Central Electricity Generating Board is causally responsible for some of the ideas I am having if I am lighting my rooms by electricity, but I am not for that reason seeing the CEGB, nor am I seeing my own brain, which is part of the causal story underlying the occurrence of visual (and other) ideas. We rule these out by the demand that an object is only seen if it resembles the ideas it causes. The CEGB does not resemble its effects, nor does my brain; and so they are unseen in this instance, though not of course generally invisible.

But the notion of resemblance is also crucial in another way. Visual/perceptual ideas have to resemble the material objects which cause them, and to resemble something is to share (some of) its qualities, to have qualities in common with it. But we have already seen that Locke takes material objects only to have a restricted range of properties. We expressed this before by saying that according to Locke material objects have the qualities of shape, size, mobility and texture (these are called the *primary* qualities), but don't have the qualities of colour and heat (these are *secondary* qualities; others are taste, feel, and resistance to touch). Now when we see a material object, our ideas have to resemble or share the properties of that object. And we might think that our ideas resemble material things in respect of their primary qualities and in respect of their secondary qualities. But Locke holds that the ideas caused in us by red objects do not resemble the objects that cause them at all. There is according to him, nothing in the object like the ideas of colour which it causes. Ideas cannot therefore fully resemble the objects which cause them, in respect of the secondary qualities at least. The material object is not like the colour of the ideas it causes, and it isn't any other colour either. But it is (or can be) like the shape of the ideas it causes; a large round object can cause a large round idea in someone looking at it.

Does this mean that material objects have no colour; that nothing out there is blue? In one way it does and in another it doesn't. They have no colour, in the sense that they do not have the properties we think of as colour; colour-as-we-see-it is an aspect of our ideas and cannot be a property of a material thing. But there is another sense in which they do have colour. We can call a material thing blue, by courtesy as it were, if it has the right sort of texture at the surface to cause the idea of blue in a perceiving mind. And Locke fastens on this last thought to avoid saying that colour is all in the mind and vanishes in the dark or when no-one is looking. If colour were entirely a property of visual ideas this is what he would have to say. But colour, viewed now as a *disposition* to cause certain distinctive ideas in us, is a permanent property of material objects, which they retain in the dark and when no-one is looking, and which they have as a result of their primary qualities. The disposition is there all the time even when it is not being triggered, and is therefore a real property of the object. But the disposition in the object does not resemble the ideas it causes in us; there is nothing in the object like our idea of colour (nor of sound, heat, taste etc.). Material objects are coloured, then, but not in the way we think of them when we imagine them or think of them as coloured.

So the macroscopic objects which constitute the physical world have the primary qualities of shape, size and mobility, and texture; and they also have secondary qualities of colour, taste, heat etc., but these last are conceived of in the objects only as dispositions to cause certain ideas in us. And now we come to a feature of Locke's thought which is absolutely crucial for all our succeeding discussions of Berkeley. Locke held that these material objects exist with their primary qualities entirely independent of any perceiving mind. Were minds entirely removed from the world, there would still be material objects existing in that world with primary qualities. It is, as it were, no thanks to us that they are there. We can have ideas of them, but the things we have ideas *of* are independently existing things whose primary qualities, at least, are nothing to do with how they appear or look to us. This is of course the view that most of us take about the world we live in. It needs a name, and can be called *realism*. Locke is a realist about material objects and their primary qualities.

Is he equally a realist about secondary qualities? In one sense he is and in another he is not. He is a realist about secondary qualities in the sense that on his view objects retain the disposition to cause ideas of colour in minds, even where there are no minds for this disposition to get a grip on. He is not a realist about secondary qualities if it is the mark of a realist to suppose that the colour of an object is nothing to do with how it looks to us or would look in other circumstances. But perhaps no-one is or ought to be a realist about colour in this last sense, for surely colour is centrally to do with how objects look.

This can help us to see that there are degrees of realism, or that realists can hold different attitudes to different properties. As I said, Locke held that physical objects exist with their primary properties entirely independent of any perceiving mind. The primary properties are held to be real properties of objects, then, in the strong sense that they exist independent of any awareness of them whatever. The secondary properties, for Locke, have a lesser degree of independence, which we could perhaps express by saying that they exist in the objects independent of any particular awareness of them. Since the secondary properties are dispositions to cause certain ideas in us, they cannot be said to be real in the strong sense. A property which is partly constituted by the nature of the ideas it causes in us can hardly be said to exist independent of all awareness. But the colour of an object, as a disposition to cause certain ideas in perceiving minds, exists there independent of any particular ideas it may happen to cause in you or me. For the object would still have had that colour even if you or I had not happened to notice it. So the secondary properties have a degree of reality, on Locke's account, but the primary ones are more real since they enjoy a greater independence.

The question of the sense in which primary and secondary properties are real and exist independent of our awareness of them will be a crucial theme in Berkeley's philosophy. He wanted to accept that both primary and secondary properties exist independent of *our* awareness of them, but still to deny the possibility of any world that is completely independent of the mind. In arguing his case he took Locke as a particularly good example of a realist. Locke's philosophy represents the most thorough attempt available to make sense of realism, that is, to provide a complete account of the world and our knowledge of it which still sees that world as existing completely independent of the mind. Realism is an enormously important and tempting way of viewing the world, and Locke's realism is a classic version. Of course some of the elements of Locke's position, as we have outlined it, may seem artificial and elaborate; but this only shows that giving a full realist account, which includes a satisfying story about the nature of and differences between the primary and the secondary qualities, is not an easy matter. Berkeley fastens on the tensions he discerns between the various parts of the realist story, and hopes thereby to demolish it entirely. But in fact he thought that every part of Locke's complex position outlined above was false; and some of it is worse than false, being literally senseless, incomprehensible or inconceivable.

We shall be considering Berkeley's positive views about the nature of the world in chapters 4 and 5, but it is worth giving a preliminary account of them here. In contrast to Locke's view that the world consists basically of tiny lumps of insensate matter, whose existence depended in no way upon the existence of any mind related to them, Berkeley held that there are only two sorts of things in the world, minds and their ideas. The physical objects of which Locke speaks are in Berkeley's view only ideas, and as ideas they can exist only in minds; they do not have and are not able to have the sort of independent existence that Locke attributes to them. It is easy to see why Berkeley's position is called *idealism*, as against Locke's realism.

In considering Berkeley's attacks on Locke, it helps to have names for the various parts of Locke's position. His theory of perception is called representative realism, because it thinks of the ideas that we perceive as somehow directly or immediately present to us and also as representing a real material world to us, a world of which we are not directly aware. Then there is the primary/secondary quality distinction. Finally there is realism pure and simple. We will take them in this order. But before beginning to consider Berkeley's objections to Locke, a caveat is called for: or rather two caveats. First, Locke's realism is not the only possible form of realism, nor is it always the most attractive. So attacks on Locke, even if successful, may not be effective as attacks on realism itself. Second, Berkeley was often mistaken about what Locke's views actually were, and wasted his attacks on a non-existent target. We shall see an instance shortly. So we shall need to keep two questions in mind. First, is this an attack on views Locke actually held? Second, if it is, is it effective against all forms of realism or only against Locke's? Although Berkeley is not always his own best advocate, and muddles one argument up with another often enough to make life difficult, we will see that his work contains some arguments and insights that do strike directly at the centre of realism, and which have left that apparently common-sense and mundane doctrine rocking ever since.

2

Realism and Representative Realism

Before examining the disagreements between Locke and Berkeley we need to point out one area of agreement which will be important for our purposes. Both are *empiricists*; they agree that all our knowledge is derived somehow from our experience. And they agree also on an account of what experience is. Our experience is seen as the flow of ideas occurring in our minds. These ideas are the things of which we are most intimately, immediately, aware. Berkeley stresses (and perhaps over-stresses) his agreement with Locke by the way he starts the *Principles*:

It is evident to any one who takes a survey of the objects of human knowledge, that they are either ideas actually imprinted on the senses, or else such as are perceived by attending to the passions and operations of the mind, or lastly ideas formed by help of memory and imagination. (P. 1)

Ideas, according to this, are the things of which we have knowledge; and they are the only things of which we know. But in this last point Berkeley goes beyond anything Locke would have said, for Locke clearly also thinks that we can have knowledge of, indeed can see, other things than ideas. In particular, Locke wants to say that we can have knowledge of material objects. Berkeley is going to deny Locke's claim that this is so in order to substitute his own account of the matter, and so he must not start out by assuming that Locke is wrong on this crucial point. The arguments that Locke is wrong here must and will come later. What they do agree on, however, is that our ideas are the only things of which we are *immediately* aware. If we know of anything else, this knowledge will be mediated by or exist in virtue of our immediate knowledge of our own ideas.

Representative realism

So, now, what has Berkeley to say against representative realism?
  His first and weakest point is that Locke's account of perception leaves it impossible for us to get any knowledge about the external world, even that there is one.

But though it were possible that solid, figured, moveable substances may exist without the mind, corresponding to the ideas we have of bodies, yet how is it possible for us to know this? (P. 18)

As we shall see, Berkeley has one central insight, which he attempts to express in various ways. This is the thought that if we are in some sense primarily aware only of our own ideas, there is a problem in how the mind goes 'beyond' its ideas to grasp the existence or even the mere possibility of anything else. There is a danger that the representative realist will imprison us in a world which consists entirely of our own ideas, leaving the material world completely beyond our reach. The argument which Berkeley offers here is an attempt to express this insight, but it is not a great success. Luckily there will be better attempts to come.

   The argument is a sceptical one: not a general sceptical argument that all knowledge is impossible, but a local sceptical argument denying the possibility of knowledge of the material world, on Locke's account. It runs as follows. Either our senses themselves reveal the existence of an external world to us, or we know of its existence by inference from what the senses do reveal to us. The senses themselves give us knowledge only of our own sensations or ideas; they do not inform us of any outer objects. But we cannot know by inference from this that there are external objects around causing the ideas of which we are aware, because it is admitted by everybody that it is perfectly possible for us to have these ideas "though no bodies existed without, resembling them" (P. 18). And we cannot say that though this is possible, still it is more probable that there are bodies than that there are not, so that though we cannot *prove* there to be a material world, we can reasonably believe that there is one. For we have no idea how such bodies, if there were any, could act upon our minds so as to imprint ideas of themselves upon them (P. 19). So Berkeley concludes his argument stirringly and with characteristic punch:

In short, if there were external bodies, it is impossible we should ever come to know it; and if there were not, we might have the very same reasons to think there were that we have now. (P. 20)

   This argument is not a success, at least as it stands, because it is not an argument against Locke's position. To see this, we need to distinguish Locke's position, which we have called representative realism, from a different position which we might call inferential realism. The inferential realist is the person Berkeley is attacking; he holds that when we perceive the objects around us we are only aware of our own ideas, and we *infer* from them the probable presence of suitable physical objects. But we are never aware of the physical objects themselves; we just work out that there must be such things, or that there probably are such things, or that the existence of such things is the best explanation for the occurrence in our minds of the ideas we have. This position differs from Locke's in a crucial way. For Locke held that our knowledge of the external world is not inferential. We *see* the world or are perceptually aware of it, though our awareness of it is mediated by a more direct awareness of something else, our ideas. Locke's theory is a 'double awareness' theory; inferential realism is a single awareness theory.

We might well wonder whether we really can make much sense of Locke's notion of a double awareness, awareness of physical objects somehow mediated by or existing in virtue of awareness of ideas. But we can already see that Berkeley's first complaint about Locke's representative realism is strictly speaking irrelevant. For Locke does not hold that the senses themselves give us knowledge only of our own sensations or ideas, and don't inform us of any outer objects.

Of course it may be that Berkeley's argument here can be reworked so as to get more of a grip on its intended target. We shall be asking whether this is so in chapter 6, when we turn to consider Berkeley's own account of our perceptual knowledge, the knowledge we get about the world by looking at it, feeling it etc.. And it is worth pointing out that though I have started Berkeley's attack on Locke with his charge that representative realism leaves perceptual knowledge impossible, for Berkeley this charge is only made late in the day, when he has already completed what he thinks of as his main assault on realism. Things are going so fast at the beginning of the *Principles* that by the time we come to sections 18–20 it is more or less all over. The fact that Berkeley leaves until so late in the day his accusation that representative realism condemns us to perceptual scepticism, reveals that he is not really too interested in it; he does not think that this is the real point, as we shall see.

However Berkeley has a second strand of argument against representative realism, which is not concerned with scepticism. This emerges in an important passage to which we shall make repeated reference:

But say you, though the ideas themselves do not exist without the mind, yet there may be things like them whereof they are copies or resemblances, which things exist without the mind, in an unthinking substance. I answer, an idea can be like nothing but an idea; a colour or figure can be like nothing but another colour or figure. If we look but ever so little into our thoughts, we shall find it impossible for us to conceive a likeness except only between our ideas. (P. 8)

This claim is a direct rejection of a central plank of Locke's representative realism, its account of the relation between an idea and an object when the idea represents the object. As we saw, Locke held that this occurs when our idea resembles the object that caused it. His account here made better sense of our perception of primary qualities than of secondary ones, because he also held that our ideas do not resemble secondary qualities as they are in the objects. But Berkeley is here attacking the account at what we might have thought was its strongest point. His attack has many layers, the simplest of which will be enough for the moment (the others will emerge later). Can we really make sense of an idea resembling a physical object in respect of its primary qualities of shape and size? The problem is that it seems hard to understand what it is like for an idea to have a size, and the notion of an idea having a shape seems equally obscure. Can one idea be bigger than another? Suppose that we think of ideas as mental pictures; these pictures have no size and no clear boundaries, and this makes it difficult to ask what shape they are either. Ideas seem to be shapeless; an idea can be an idea *of* a square object without being square itself, and this not because it has some other shape, just as an idea can be an idea of a jagged or furry object without itself having any such property. So the crucial concept in representative realism, the account of representation in terms of resemblance, fails to deliver what we want. We can't suppose that our ideas resemble physical objects in respect of those qualities, the primary ones, that are essential to Locke's physical world. (Interestingly, however, the notion of a resemblance between idea and object seems to make more sense in the case of the secondary qualities; our ideas may seem actually to have the property of colour, in respect of which they would be able to resemble physical objects if Locke had not already decided that colour in the objects is only a power in them to cause those ideas in us.)

One might reasonably think that this point is so obvious that Locke could not possibly have missed it, and that he must really have held some more subtle view. Don't we all know that pictures (to take the hardest case) can represent objects to which they bear not the slightest resemblance? Indeed we do, and so did Locke, I imagine. But the only remarks he makes in the *Essay* do seem to express the view that representation can only be achieved by a resemblance between the representer and the represented. To improve on the theory we have attributed to him, we would have to find an account of resemblance which does not hold that two objects can only resemble each other if they share some property. But no such account is even hinted at in Locke. So Berkeley's argument, if successful, is decisive against representative realism as Locke presents it. But it would be powerless against a different version of representative realism, which gave a different account of representation. It is the use of the notion of resemblance which Berkeley takes to be the weak point.

The distinction between primary and secondary qualities

This distinction divides the properties of physical objects into two sorts, and claims to justify a divisive attitude towards them. Locke takes the primary qualities more seriously than he takes the secondary. Realism may come in degrees, but Locke reserves the most extreme form for the primary qualities. The primary qualities of objects are those that they would retain in the absence of all relations with perceiving minds. When we conceive of the world from our own viewpoint, we have a *relative* conception of it which includes the ascription of secondary qualities to physical objects. But we can also achieve an *absolute* conception of how the world would be, independent of any relation to ourselves or other minds, and in this conception the primary qualities are present without the secondary.[1]

unimaginable but not inconceivable

Berkeley rejects Locke's separation of the primary from the secondary. Unfortunately he takes it that according to Locke the secondary qualities exist only in the mind.

They who assert that figure, motion, and the rest of the primary or original qualities do exist without the mind, in unthinking substances, do at the same time acknowledge that colours, sounds, heat, cold, and such like secondary qualities, do not, which they tell us are sensations existing in the mind alone, that depend on and are occasioned by the different size, texture and motion of the minute particles of matter. (P. 10)

But though this affects what happens once the distinction between primary and secondary has been collapsed, it does not directly vitiate his argument against the distinction. The argument is that we cannot conceive of the primary qualities existing without the secondary qualities.

I desire anyone to reflect and try, whether he can by any abstraction of thought, conceive the extension and motion of a body, without all other sensible qualities. For my own part, I see evidently that it is not in my power to frame an idea of a body extended and moved, but I must withal give it some colour or other sensible quality which is acknowledged to exist only in the mind. In short, extension, figure, and motion, abstracted from all other qualities, are inconceivable. (P. 10)

The argument is that the secondary qualities are *inextricable* from the primary ones, but it is not easy to see in exactly what sense Berkeley thinks this is so. He might mean that the secondary qualities are so

---

[1] For the idea of the absolute conception see B. Williams *Descartes: The Project of Pure Enquiry* (Harmondsworth: Penguin Books 1978), pp. 64–7 and 244–9.

central to our way of thinking of the world that we cannot hive them off and conceive of what the world would be like without them; we can achieve a relative conception of the world, but an absolute conception is beyond us. If this were so, it would be pointless to claim that though *we* cannot achieve an absolute conception of the world, still the world might be as the absolute conception conceives it to be. For Berkeley would rightly reply that if we cannot attain the absolute conception, we cannot understand the suggestion that the world should be as that conception conceives it, and so anyone who holds that this might be so is contending for something that he does not understand, But why, exactly, are the secondary qualities inextricable from the primary? Can't we conceive of a world of objects which only have the qualities of shape, size, texture and motion?

Unimaginable

One suggestion might be that what is wrong with this is that we cannot conceive of what such a world would look like. The way our world looks to us is dominated by colour; the outlines of objects are outlines of their colour (including here black and white). What would things look like if they had no colour? But defenders of the possibility of an absolute conception would presumably say that they are not in the business of saying what the world, as it conceives, would look like; what they are telling us is what it would *be* like. But could the world be in ways it couldn't look? Our world can do this, but we can only make sense of this because we can understand how the properties it would then have fit in with properties that do present themselves to us. We can't make the required sense of a world which is entirely unpresentable.

At the moment this is all speculation. We are not going to make much progress in understanding Berkeley's reasons for the inextricability thesis until we have discovered what he means by the phrase "by any abstraction of thought" in the passage quoted above, and this will have to wait until the next chapter. There are, however, other Berkeleian arguments against the primary/secondary distinction.

The first of these is found in the First Dialogue, where Berkeley makes a more detailed attack on the distinction, one which is more independent of his other views. One reason for being impressed by the distinction is the feeling that there is such a thing as a correct answer to the question what the real size and shape of an object is, but not to the question what its real colour is. Objects look different colours in different lights, and although we may prefer to think in terms of the colour they look in ordinary daylight, this preference is more a fact about us than about the objects. But we do think that objects have a real shape and size, in virtue of which they do sometimes look the shape and size they really are.

Berkeley attacks this way of thinking by asking at what distance and to what ?

what sort of mind objects look their true size. Objects look smaller and larger as we move towards them or away from them, and something that looks very small to us may look enormous to a mite. It is no answer to this question to say that we discover the real size of an object not by looking at it but by measuring it; we say that this object is nine inches long, and think of this as its true or real size. It is true that size is perfectly reasonably measured in feet and inches, but this is irrelevant to the question because we now ask in what conditions an inch looks an inch long. There seems to be no answer to this question other than one analogous to the answer we gave in the case of colour; inches look an inch long at a normal working distance from the eye, or something like that. So the notion of the true size of an object has no status different from or higher than that of its true colour. Objects have no more and no less one than they have the other.

But perhaps the most telling argument against the primary/secondary distinction derives from a thought that we have already seen used in Berkeley's attack on representative realism, his claim that an idea can resemble nothing but another idea. This claim about what can resemble what is fatal to the distinction as Locke draws it; it gets a grip because Locke expresses the distinction in terms of resemblance, of the ability of our ideas to resemble objects in respect of the primary qualities but not of the secondary qualities. And we have already argued that Locke cannot make this claim good; our ideas cannot resemble material objects in respect of their primary qualities. This means that on Locke's account, since he has already given up the thought that ideas might resemble objects in respect of their secondary qualities, our ideas cannot resemble objects at all. But this is disastrous to the hope of showing how our thought gets to fit the world or how we capture in our conception the way that world is. Our thought emerges as unable to correspond to the way the world is. But this is impossible, or at least if possible it is not something we can make much sense of. The only world we can make sense of is one which our ideas can fit (resemble). If the realist's world is one which our ideas cannot fit, then so much the worse for it.

What is effectively the same point can be made in another way. The properties of ideas are essentially to do with the ways in which things can appear to us. But Locke is claiming that some of the properties of our ideas are properties which they can share with objects, and which those objects are held to retain in the absolute conception of the world. But this is impossible, because the absolute conception conceives of the world in ways from which appearance has been entirely extracted. If the relevant properties of ideas are essentially phenomenal, i.e. to do with how things *appear* to us, it is not possible to conceive that objects other than ideas might bear those properties in worlds where there is no such thing as

concerned with sight only
what of touch

appearance. Properties of objects, then, conceived absolutely, are not properties that ideas could have. It follows again that we cannot attain the absolute conception of the world, for we are trying to conceive of objects in ways which both are and are not to do with the way in which they can appear to us.

This way of putting the point amounts to stripping off yet another layer from the doctrine that an idea can resemble nothing but another idea.

Locke is not justified, then, in his preferentially realist attitude towards the primary qualities. The qualities of the world, as we experience them, are all of a piece. Berkeley concludes from this that since the secondary qualities are acknowledged to exist only in the mind, the primary ones can only exist in the mind too. But this is a mistake, as we have seen. Locke never held that the secondary qualities exist only in the mind, and so Berkeley's dramatic idealist conclusion cannot be simply extracted in this direct way from the breakdown of the primary/secondary distinction. What is more, there are other ways of drawing that distinction, as we shall see in chapter 6; Locke's form of realism is not the only form, and it may be that a non-Lockean version of the difference between primary and secondary qualities will be immune to Berkeley's objections.

But Berkeley has other ways of reaching his main, idealist conclusion. So we now turn to look at his direct attack on Locke's realism.

Locke's realism

Here we consider three Berkeleian arguments that share a common purpose. Berkeley's text contains many strands of argument against the realist view that the physical world has an existence independent of any relation to perceiving minds, and to focus on three separable ones in this way is to some extent to distort his thought. There may, however, be no other way in.

The first argument is found at the beginning of the *Principles*:

It is indeed an opinion strangely prevailing amongst men, that houses, mountains, rivers, and in a word all sensible objects have an existence natural or real, distinct from their being perceived by the understanding. But with how great an assurance and acquiescence soever this principle may be entertained in the world; yet whoever shall find it in his heart to call it in question, may, if I mistake not, perceive it to involve a manifest contradiction. For what are the forementioned objects but the things we perceive by sense, and what do we perceive besides our own ideas or sensations; and is it not plainly repugnant that any one of these or any combination of them should exist unperceived? (P. 4)

This argument will hardly suffice to deprive the physical world of independent reality, and I doubt that Berkeley thought that it could. It seems to argue to a conclusion that physical objects cannot exist unperceived from two premises:

1 physical objects are the things we perceive by sense

and

2 ideas and sensations are the things we perceive by sense.

Of course the conclusion does follow from these premises, since the premises entail that physical objects are ideas or sensations, which cannot exist unperceived. The problem here is not that the argument is invalid, but that nobody in their right mind would accept both of the premises. For to do so is to accept that the relation we bear to the physical objects we perceive is identical to the relation we bear to our own ideas and sensations. Now this might be the conclusion of some argument, but it can hardly be viewed as an uncontestable starting point. Certainly Locke would not accept both 1 and 2; he would be far more careful (in his better moments), holding rather that we *have* ideas and perceive objects, or alternatively that we perceive ideas and *see* objects. In this way he would, or at least could, be careful to mark a difference in relation by a difference in terminology. So this argument of Berkeley's is ineffective as an argument against realism, since it starts from a position which no realist would admit. The argument may express Berkeley's views, but it provides no argument for them.

The second strand of argument derives yet again from the doctrine that an idea can resemble nothing but another idea. If this is true, and if to conceive of an object is to have an idea which resembles it, it follows that we cannot conceive of anything other than an idea. Ideas are of course dependent both for their existence and for their qualities on the minds that have them. According to the realist, physical objects are not; they have an existence and a nature independent of any relation to perceiving minds. And this means that the realist's physical world is inconceivable; since our ideas cannot resemble that world, we cannot conceive of it. We can make no sense of the suggestion that there should or could be such a thing. It is not just that for all we know there might not be one; rather we know that there can't be one, because we know that the suggestion that there is one makes no sense.

It is worth stressing the strength of this result. It reveals a constant feature of Berkeley's rejection of realism. Earlier in this chapter we considered a sceptical argument to the effect that since we are only aware

of our own ideas there may for all we know be no physical world outside
them and causing them. We rejected this argument as weak, but Berkeley
also would think of it as weak; for to say that for all we know there is no
such thing as the realist's physical world is tacitly to admit that we do at
least understand what it would be like for there to be one. But it is this
last idea that is Berkeley's real target. So strongly does he want to stress
his view that realism is incomprehensible that he is willing to grant that
were it only comprehensible it would be true. Thus he writes:

I am content to put the whole upon this issue; if you can but conceive it possible
for one extended moveable substance, or in general, for any one idea or any thing
like an idea, to exist otherwise than in a mind perceiving it, I shall readily give up
the cause: and as for all that *compages* of external bodies which you contend for, I
shall grant its existence, though you cannot either give me any reason why you
believe it exists, or assign any use to it when it is supposed to exist. I say, the bare
possibility of your opinion's being true, shall pass for an argument that it is so. (P.
22)

If Berkeley's central claim is that realism is incomprehensible, it
follows that various defences that might occur to the realist are irrelevant.
This matters because these defences are exactly the ones that realists do
commonly offer to what they take to be Berkeley's main point. Realists
are prone to say that they do have some reason for believing that there
exists an independent material world, a reason founded perhaps in their
ability to *see* that world. Alternatively (either as an explanation of the first
point or in addition to it) they claim that we need to suppose that there
exists an independent world in order to provide the richest and most
powerful explanation of our experience. Why is it that things appear to
me in a certain way? The realist answer is always that there exist real
independent material objects in my vicinity, which are having a certain
effect on my senses. This is a very plausible and promising answer. But it
is not an answer to Berkeley. It is irrelevant to Berkeley's main point, and
so cannot itself stand as a satisfactory defence of realism against idealist
attacks.

Berkeley is in fact willing to take the realist on even on his own ground.
He argues forcefully that the realist's real objects will not in fact serve to
provide the explanation of which realists are so proud. He says:

they own themselves unable to comprehend in what manner body can act upon
spirit, or how it is possible it should imprint any idea in the mind. Hence it is
evident the production of ideas or sensations in our minds, can be no reason why
we should suppose matter or corporeal substances, since that is acknowledged to
remain equally inexplicable with, or without this supposition. (P. 19)

Berkeley wants to win every argument. His point that it is not clear how matter can act upon mind is a reasonable one, but perhaps he exaggerates when he says that the realist explanation of experience is no explanation at all. Later (in chapters 7 and 8) we will see him arguing instead that he can provide as good an explanation as any realist can, without any need to invoke the existence of matter. This is a better position, whether or not it is in the end successful. But it is important to remember that whatever our decision on that point, Berkeley's main argument does not concern the usefulness or otherwise of matter in explanation, but simply whether we can understand the realist's talk of independent material objects at all. If we cannot, there is simply no question whether postulating the existence of such things provides an effective explanation of anything. And the realist's attempt to defend himself by saying that we need to postulate the existence of matter just begs the question against Berkeley, since it assumes the point at issue by taking it for granted that the notion of an independent material object makes sense.

In general we can distinguish two sorts of sceptical argument. First is the weak sort given above which admits that we understand some proposition but holds that we never know whether it is true or false. Second is the strong sort that holds that we do not even understand the proposition, and so *a fortiori* cannot have any evidence in favour of it. Berkeley's argument may be seen as sceptical, but his scepticism about realism is always of the strong sort; it is a scepticism about understanding and not about evidence or knowledge. Such arguments have a strength and a weakness. The weakness is that they are not matters of degree; it is all or nothing, and there is a danger of its being nothing. The strength is that they are quickly effective if effective at all; this is why Berkeley, after having taken (as he thinks) only ten pages of text to demolish the idea that the physical world exists independent of mind, feels the need to apologise for having been so long about it:

I am afraid I have given cause to think me needlessly prolix in handling this subject. For to what purpose is it to dilate on that which may be demonstrated with the utmost evidence in a line or two, to any one that is capable of the least reflection? (P. 22)

Berkeley's third argument against realism, which is apparently independent of the second, occurs most clearly in the First Dialogue. Philonous represents Berkeley:

PHILONOUS: I am content to put the whole upon this issue. If you can

*but thats, I
we cannot conceive
of it*

conceive it possible for any mixture or combination of qualities, or any sensible object whatever, to exist without the mind, then I will grant it actually to be so.

HYLAS: If it comes to that, the point will soon be decided. What more easy than to conceive a tree or house existing by itself, independent of, and unperceived by any mind whatsoever? I do at this present time conceive them existing after that manner.

PHILONOUS: How say you, Hylas, can you see a thing which is at the same time unseen?

HYLAS: No, that were a contradiction.

PHILONOUS: Is it not as great a contradiction to talk of *conceiving* a thing which is *unconceived*?

HYLAS: It is.

PHILONOUS: The tree or house therefore which you think of, is conceived by you.

HYLAS: How should it be otherwise?

PHILONOUS: And what is conceived, is surely in the mind.

HYLAS: Without question, that which is conceived is in the mind.

PHILONOUS: How then came you to say, you conceived a house or tree existing independent and out of all minds, whatsoever?

HYLAS: That was I own an oversight; but stay, let me consider what led me into it. – It is a pleasant mistake enough. As I was thinking of a tree in a solitary place, where no one was present to see it, methought that was to conceive a tree as existing unperceived or unthought of, not considering that I myself conceived it all the while. But now I plainly see, that all I can do is to frame ideas in my own mind. I may indeed conceive in my own thoughts the idea of a tree, or a house, or a mountain, but this is all. And this is far from proving, that I can conceive them *existing out of the minds of all spirits.* (p. 200)

It is lovely to see Hylas' ingenuousness in this passage, but in many ways he represents just the reply we are all tempted to make to Berkeley until we see why it is irrelevant. We are so used to thinking of the physical world as independent of ourselves that we find it hard to accept the suggestion that there might be something wrong or even dubious about this idea.

Berkeley claims here not only to provide a refutation of realism but also to offer a diagnosis of the realist's mistake. The argument is that in claiming to conceive of physical objects as existing unconceived, the realist is contradicting himself in as gross a way as if he had claimed to be able to see something which is at the same time unseen. And if this were true we could easily see why Berkeley thought that realism involved a particularly crude and obvious error. Unfortunately for Berkeley, we shall see that it is not true.

The diagnosis does have something to offer, even so. For what it shows is that the realist conception of the world is not simply a conception of a world that nobody is looking at. In conceiving of a tree standing alone in a field, I conceive of it from some point of view, of what it looks like from some angle. But the realist should be offering to conceive of a tree which doesn't look in any way at all, which doesn't appear to anyone. And this is not such an easy conception to achieve, even if Berkeley has not shown that it is impossible.

What is wrong with Berkeley's attempt to draw an analogy between conceiving an unconceived tree, one that exists out of all minds, and seeing an unseen tree? One suggestion has been that Berkeley is thinking of conceiving as the creation of little pictures or images in the mind; this is commonly called an imagist theory of conception. What Berkeley is arguing is that we cannot have a picture in our mind of a tree of which there is no picture in anyone's mind. And the supposed mistake here is to take it that because every picture of a tree must be a picture of the tree from some point of view, we cannot have a conception of the tree except as seen from some point of view. It is as if to conceive of a tree is to imagine perceiving a tree, i.e. to create for yourself an idea which a tree might have created. Since in perception objects are presented to us from a point of view, conceiving would on this account essentially involve the notion of a point of view; to conceive of an object would be to think of it as it would appear from some point of view. And it is suggested that this imagist theory of conception is wrong, on the grounds that we can conceive of all sorts of things without having little pictures of them in our minds. This is particularly obvious in the case of things of which there *cannot* be pictures, such as the number one or friendship or danger. And if the theory is wrong, Berkeley has no grounds for arguing that any conception of a tree must conceive of it as seen from some point of view. For his attack relied on thinking of conceiving as picturing.[2]

In my view this criticism is less than telling. First, the question whether we can imagine such a tree is relevant, as we saw in discussing Berkeley's attack on the primary-secondary distinction; for it began to seem problematic that we had no idea what the world, as the absolute conception conceives it, would look like. Second, Berkeley's real point is that we cannot have a conception in our mind of something of which there is no conception in anyone's mind because the very idea of doing so is contradictory. He asks "Is it not as great a contradiction to talk of conceiving a thing which is unconceived?" and the answer to this question does not depend on whether or not we take conceiving on the model of picturing. Despite appearances, there can be a picture of a tree of which there is no picture.

Berkeley's claim is that it is a contradiction to hold that I can conceive

[2] See (e.g.) C. McGinn *The Subjective View* (Oxford: Clarendon Press 1983), pp. 80–1.

of something existing unconceived, just as it is to hold that I can see something that is unseen. The first mistake here is that this is irrelevant as an attack on the realist. The realist could admit it to be contradictory to say that one conceives a tree which exists unconceived, but hold that this doesn't affect his position. For what he is saying is that he can conceive of a tree that *could* exist unconceived, not one that does. Indeed this is the very claim that Berkeley should be challenging, because he has allowed (P. 22) that the mere possibility of realism is enough to establish realism as true, and this is all that the realist is here claiming. And there is nothing contradictory about this claim, any more than there is about the similar claim to see a tree that could exist unseen.

But Berkeley's argument here is worse than irrelevant; it is invalid. There is no analogy between seeing and conceiving of the sort he is trying to draw. And this means that it is not contradictory to say that one conceives of something existing unconceived. The important thing here is to distinguish between conceiving of something that is existing unconceived and conceiving of something *as* existing unconceived. When we talk about conceiving of something *as* having some property we are talking about the way we conceive that thing to be, not about the way it is; and we can conceive it to have all sorts of properties which in fact it has not got. So the fact that the thing is in fact conceived by us does not show that we cannot be conceiving of it *as* unconceived.

There is admittedly a distinction between seeing a tree and seeing something *as* a tree, just as there is between seeing a threat and seeing something as a threat. And it may be that for special reasons we cannot see something as unseen. But this is not because of the contradiction Berkeley thought he was appealing to; it is rather to do with the sorts of ways in which we can represent objects to ourselves.

So the three arguments we have considered have not been very successful. The most effective has been that deriving from the by now familiar thought that an idea can resemble nothing but another idea. We may reasonably wonder whether this thought is strong enough to overthrow the realist belief in a world existing independent of all minds. Nonetheless I think that Berkeley's strongest argument is a version of the First Dialogue argument about the unconceived tree. Berkeley has misled us by his talk of a contradiction, and we have argued against him by showing that there is no contradiction in the case. But the thrust of all this depends on what is meant by a contradiction. We are nowadays familiar with a strict use of this term deriving from formal logic, but Berkeley knew nothing of this; his notion of a contradiction is much vaguer than ours. And we shall see at the end of the next chapter that there is another way of taking the First Dialogue argument, which reveals the true basis of Berkeley's position. But to do this we need to make a

detour. I said of the first of the three arguments against the
between primary and secondary qualities that we would make
headway with it until we understood what Berkeley meant
abstraction. The notion of abstraction is central in Berkeley's r
realism. Immediately after his first attempt to refute the realist, he writes:

If we thoroughly examine this tenet, it will, perhaps, be found at bottom to
depend on the doctrine of *abstract ideas*. For can there be a nicer strain of
abstraction than to distinguish the existence of sensible objects from their being
perceived, so as to conceive them existing unperceived? (P. 5)

It will be the task of the next chapter to make sense of this introduction
of the notion of abstraction. It is crucial to Berkeley's metaphysics in a
way that many readers of Berkeley have missed. Meanwhile the present
chapter has been concerned to distinguish between good and bad
Berkeleian arguments against representative realism as a theory of
perception, against Locke's version of the distinction between primary
and secondary qualities and against realism itself. We found that
Berkeley is capable of producing bad or irrelevant arguments in all these
three areas, but that he offers more promising thoughts as well.
Interestingly, the claim that an idea can resemble nothing but another
idea played a role in each of the three areas, which shows its importance.
It raises difficulties for the representative realist's account of representation as resemblance, for the possibility of an absolute conception in
which we are to conceive of the world as devoid of appearance, and for
the realist's attempt to conceive of something which is not an idea. In the
next chapter we shall have to ask how Berkeley's use of the claim that an
idea can resemble nothing but another idea is related to his thoughts
about abstraction.

Perhaps the most important thing that has emerged so far is that
Berkeley's main complaint against realism is that its account of the world
as independent of mind is impossible because it is inconceivable. It is this
very strong claim, rather than the weaker one that we have no evidence
that there is any such world, that Berkeley's account of abstraction must
be intended to establish.

3

Abstraction

Berkeley devotes the Introduction to the *Principles* almost entirely to an attack on Locke's account of abstract general ideas. This in itself reveals the importance he attaches to the role of abstraction in philosophical thought. He presents the matter as if his interest in abstraction is an interest in the nature of language, since as we shall see Locke uses that notion in his account of language. But in fact Berkeley thinks that misuse of the notion of abstraction has caused errors elsewhere; it leads us not only to make mistakes about language but to make mistakes in language as well.

Locke's theory of abstraction

Locke introduces the notion of abstraction to resolve a puzzle that arises in the investigation of the different sorts of words that go together to make up the sentences in our language. Among other words, there are names for things. And there are two sorts of names. First there are names for particular things, which we nowadays call proper names: the name 'London', for example, or the name 'Boris Becker'. Second, there are what Locke calls 'general' names, which name several different things equally well; examples are the name 'man' and 'horse'. Locke faces a problem about how there can be such general names, because of his account of what it is for a word to have a meaning. According to Locke, words only have meanings if they stand for ideas in the mind of the person using them. Locke would say that I can think about London without using the *word* 'London', as when I have an idea of London in my mind, an idea which resembles London and can therefore represent it to me. But if I think in words or speak out loud, my words only have a meaning if they stand for or go proxy for an idea of London in my mind. Which of course they normally do. There are however beings that can utter words but for whom those words are meaningless. A parrot, for instance, is a being for whom words are meaningless shapes or sounds.

Now what sort of ideas do names stand for? Proper names stand for ideas of particular objects; the name 'London' stands for the idea of

London in my mind, an idea which can have any detail that London does. London, at least, can resemble my idea entirely. But what ideas do general names stand for? The general name 'man' cannot stand for the idea of any particular man, for if it did it would be a proper name of that man and not a general name of all men equally. Do we have any other ideas than those of particular objects? If not, general names are impossible because there are no ideas for them to stand for.

Locke raises and answers the question in this way:

The next thing to be considered is *how general words come to be made*. For since all things that exist are only particulars, how come we by general terms, or where find we those general natures they are supposed to stand for? Words become general by being made the signs of general *ideas*; and *ideas* become general by separating from them the circumstances of time and place and any other *ideas* that may determine them to this or that particular existence. By this way of abstraction they are made capable of representing more individuals than one: each of which, having in it a conformity to that abstract *idea*, is (as we call it) of that sort. (*Essay*, bk. 3, ch.3, sec.6; henceforth simply 3.3.6)

Locke's theory is that to start off with (or as children) we have only ideas of particular objects – particular men, for example. Such particular objects as we have ideas of, we may have names for too: the name 'Daddy', perhaps, would be one.

Afterwards, when time and a larger acquaintance have made them observe that there are a great many other things in the world that, in some common agreements of shape and several other qualities, resemble their father and mother and those persons they have been used to, they frame an *idea* which they find those many particulars do partake in, and to that they give, with others, the name *man*, for example. And *thus they come to have a general name*, and a general *idea*. Wherein they make nothing new, but only leave out of the complex *idea* they had of *Peter* and *James*, *Mary* and *Jane* that which is peculiar to each, and retain only what is common to them all. (*Essay* 3.3.7)

So Locke holds that we move from ideas of particular objects, each of which can only stand for that one object, to general ideas which can stand for any or all objects of a certain sort indifferently, by the process of abstraction. Abstraction is subtraction; we subtract from a group of similar ideas of particular things all those elements in respect of which they (or their objects) are different, creating a new shorn idea whose content is only those elements common to all the original ideas of particular objects.

Abstract ideas, so created, must be less rich and complex than ideas of particular objects. An idea of a particular object probably contains a reference to what Locke calls 'circumstances of time and place'; that is, the idea is of the object as having been at such and such a place at such and such a time. Since no two objects can be in the same place at the same time, such elements restrict any complex idea that contains them to one particular object. Such elements must therefore be removed from our ideas of particular objects in the formation of an abstract general idea.

Each abstract idea is of course in itself particular; its generality lies not so much in its nature as in the use to which we put it, which is to stand indifferently for any or all objects of the same sort. General ideas *must* be formed by abstraction if they are to serve this purpose, Locke argues, because only such artificially shorn ideas would be able to resemble and hence stand for more than one object.

So in answer to the question how there can be general names, common to more than one object, Locke holds that such names stand for special ideas formed by abstraction, which though particular in themselves are able to be general in their signification.

Berkeley's reply

Berkeley's first attempt is to argue that abstraction as Locke describes it requires us to conceive separately qualities that cannot exist separately, and that this is impossible.

I own myself able to abstract in one sense, as when I consider some particular parts or qualities separated from others, with which though they are united in some object, yet, it is possible they may really exist without them. But I deny that I can abstract one from another, or conceive separately, those qualities which it is impossible should exist so separated; or that I can frame a general notion by abstracting from particulars in the manner aforesaid. (PI. 10)

But this is not a very good way of getting at Locke, because abstraction as Locke conceives it will never require us to conceive separately qualities that cannot exist separately, and so the question whether this is impossible or not is irrelevant. The process of abstraction, for Locke, requires us to retain from the original ideas of particular objects all elements common to all. If two qualities necessarily exist together, then if one is common to all relevant objects the other will be. We shall never be forced by this to conceive separately two qualities that cannot exist separately; any properly formed abstract general idea will contain either both or neither.

However the thoughts with which Berkeley concluded the passage quoted above contain a rather different suggestion. He writes:

I can imagine a man with two heads or the upper parts of a man joined to the body of a horse. I can consider the hand, the eye, the nose, each by itself abstracted or separated from the rest of the body. But then whatever hand or eye I imagine, it must have some particular shape and colour. Likewise the idea of man that I frame to myself, must be either of a white, or a black, or a tawny, a straight, or a crooked, a tall or a low, or a middle-sized man. I cannot by any effort of thought conceive the abstract idea above described. (PI. 10)

And this prompts rather different considerations. On Locke's account, when we form the abstract idea of man we are forced by the fact that different men are different colours to eliminate from the abstract idea mention of any particular colour. But all men have at least this in common, that they have some colour or other, and *this* feature must obviously be part of any general idea of man. We can express this more clearly using the distinction between determinate and determinable. A determinable is a property like colour or height of which one can have determinate values; one can be determinately white or black, six foot three or five foot eight. And what Berkeley is saying is that Locke's abstract general ideas will in many cases be phrased in terms of determinables rather than in terms of determinate values of those determinables. In the case of men, as we have seen, we will have to include in our general idea the elements of having some colour and height, but not any particular colour or height. And this is what Berkeley claims to be impossible. According to him, I cannot frame an idea of an object which has some colour or other but no particular colour, and yet this absurdity is what Locke's abstractors are trying to achieve. It sounds even more absurd when expressed as the attempt to form an idea of a thing which has some particular colour but no colour in particular.

Is this as impossible as it seems? I think the best way to answer this question is to consider how Berkeley would reply to attempts to defend Locke on this point.

A common defence of Locke here is to repeat the charge we have seen earlier that Berkeley is misled by his adherence to the imagist theory of conception.[1] On this complaint, Berkeley is seen as influenced by the thought that there cannot be a picture or image of a hand of no particular colour, and hence persuades himself that we cannot conceive of a hand in such a way. But Berkeley's position need not be taken in this way. On his own showing, the problem does not in the first place concern our inability to conceive of an object in any single way, but rather a supposed inability to conceive of it in one way and not in another, when the two are necessarily present or absent together in the way in which determinate

[1] See (e.g.) G. Pitcher *Berkeley* (London: Routledge and Kegan Paul 1977), p. 67.

and determinable go necessarily together. The problem is not that we cannot conceive of a hand of no particular colour, but rather that we cannot conceive of a hand which has some particular colour but no particular colour: a hand that has only determinable colour.

One might think that a line drawing of a hand is a representation of a hand that is coloured (since all hands are) but has no particular colour. But Berkeley would reply that this is a confusion. Colour is not represented here at all; the representation is not of a hand which is coloured, and if it were it would have to be of a hand which has some particular colour. And this is because the line drawing does not represent the hand *as* coloured but having no particular colour. Berkeley's point is that this dual representation is impossible. And we can be led from this to wonder what it would be like to represent an object as having no particular colour. With this question the impossibility of a dual re-presentation of the object as coloured but having no particular colour begins to reveal a single impossibility. For how could any drawing represent its object as having no particular colour?

Putting the matter in this way, and using the example of a drawing, may encourage us still to think that Berkeley's point here is simply one about picturing. But it is not. The charge is that there is no way in which we can represent an object to ourselves as having no particular colour. It is not of course good enough in response to this simply to repeat to oneself the words 'I conceive of this object as having no particular colour'. One needs to attain a positive conception of an object as having no particular colour, and it is not clear how moving away from the pictorial is supposed to help.

But is Locke really committed to saying that this is possible? Would it not be sufficient to say that we can conceive of a hand of no particular colour, by simply omitting to put any reference to colour into our abstract general ideas of a hand and of man? The attraction of this line is that if it works, it enables us to say how we can achieve the absolute conception of the world despite Berkeley's doubts. For what we are doing counts equally as conceiving of a hand of no colour at all, in the way which that conception seems to require. But this reveals what is wrong with this suggestion. Locke's account of abstraction prevents us from omitting all mention of colour from our abstract idea of a hand, because colour, conceived determinably, is something that all hands have in common. This is not a way, therefore, in which Locke could claim to be able to achieve the absolute conception of the world.

The real point is that in the absolute conception we are trying to conceive of the world positively *as having no colour*. A mere failure to mention colour would mean that when we add colour to our original conception we don't need to change what is there already. But the absolute conception is one from which colour is explicitly excluded, and would need to be changed rather than supplemented if we were now to include colour again. In general, the idea of representing the absence of colour by simply failing to mention colour is no use – any more than we represent something as having no particular age by failing to represent it as having some particular age.

Another hope would be to say that Berkeley has made the mistake of holding that since every hand must be some particular colour, we cannot conceive of a hand of no particular colour. For we would be attempting to conceive of a hand in a way in which no hand could possibly be. If Berkeley were to have argued in this way, he would be wrong; for we know perfectly well that we are able to conceive of objects in ways in which they neither are nor could be. But this defence of Locke fails also. Berkeley is not trying to say that since hands must *be* this way, we cannot conceive of them in any other way. His point is one about the impossibility of conceiving of a hand in two ways at once, viz. as having some particular colour and no particular colour.

Berkeley's point was originally expressed as the claim that we cannot conceive of a hand that has no particular colour. But in the subsequent discussion it has been extended in two ways which will be important. First, the reasons for which it is impossible to conceive of a hand that has no particular colour were also reasons why it is impossible to conceive of a hand that is *able* to have no particular colour, and why it is impossible to conceive of a hand *as* having no particular colour. None of these ways of conceiving of hands is available to us.

Can an idea be general without being abstract?

Locke held that an idea could not be general, i.e. stand for more than one thing, unless it was abstract, i.e. formed by the process of abstraction. This was because only abstract ideas were shorn of 'considerations of time and place', which bound them to one particular object. All other ideas, those which occur naturally in the mind, are ideas which can only represent one particular object.

Berkeley's view, as we have seen, is that Locke's process involves an incoherence. Does this mean that he thinks that general ideas are impossible, agreeing with Locke that to be general an idea must be abstract? Or does he rather hold that general ideas are possible, because a general idea need not for that reason be abstract? Or, finally, does he think that Locke's insistence on the need for general ideas to make sense of the ability of a single word to name more than one object is mistaken?

Berkeley's eventual position is complex. He holds that ideas *can* be general without being abstract, but that words can have what we may call a general significance without the intermediary of any general idea. The first of these two thoughts, that we may have general ideas which are not abstract, is stressed thus:

And here it is to be noted that I do not deny absolutely there are general ideas, but only that there are any *abstract general ideas*. (PI. 12)

And he continues:

an idea, which considered in itself is particular, becomes general, by being made to represent or stand for all other particular ideas of the same sort. To make this plain by an example, suppose a geometrician is demonstrating the method, of cutting a line in two equal parts. He draws, for instance, a black line of an inch in length, this which in itself is a particular line is nevertheless with regard to its signification general, since as it is there used, it represents all particular lines whatsoever; so that what is demonstrated of it, is demonstrated of all lines, or, in other words, of a line in general. And as that particular line becomes general, by being made a sign, so the name *line* which taken absolutely is particular, by being a sign is made general. And as the former owes its generality, not to its being the sign of an abstract or general line, but of all particular right lines that may possibly exist, so the latter must be thought to derive its generality from the same cause, namely, the various particular lines which it indifferently denotes.

It is important to be clear here about exactly what Berkeley is saying. He is saying, first, that an entirely particular idea can be made general, by being used to stand for all objects of a certain sort. But he is denying the more important part of the doctrine of abstract ideas, which is that the generality of words can only derive from the generality of ideas. One could make the mistake of saying that in the passage above Berkeley is arguing that a particular idea is made general by being made to stand for all other ideas of the same sort, and that a word is made general by being associated with just such an idea. But in fact things are the other way round. Berkeley is really arguing that the way ideas are made general is exactly the same way that words are made general, and so that the generality of words is not mediated by the prior generality of ideas. Anything, word, idea or object, can become general if we choose to use it as a sign for all objects of the same sort. As he says, "an idea . . . becomes general by being made to . . . stand for all other particular *ideas* of the same sort", and a line becomes general by being used to "represent all particular *lines* whatsoever" (my emphasis). The analogy with words is not perfect, for a word does not become general by being made to stand for all other *words* of the same sort. But that is just the point. What Berkeley is stressing is that just as a particular line or a particular idea can be general in its signification, when we use it to stand for all objects of a certain sort, so a general word, e.g. "line", "must be thought to derive its generality from the same cause, namely, the *various particular* lines it indifferently denotes".

We might be excused error on this point, for Berkeley is not as helpful in expressing his position as he might be. Thus in the preceding section he writes:

a word becomes general by being made the sign, not of an abstract general idea but, of several particular ideas, any one of which it indifferently suggests to the mind. (PI. 11)

Here Berkeley says that a general word is one which stands for several particular ideas at once, not one special one. But he need not be read as saying that this is the only way in which words can get to be general. As far as this goes it is open to him to say more directly that a general word is one which is made the sign of a number of particular objects indifferently, be those objects ideas or things. We can admit that if we can use a particular idea in this general way we can do the same with a word, without admitting that a word can only be used this way if it is used to stand for a particular idea that we are using this way, or for ideas at all. Instead, Berkeley is saying that anything whatever, line, idea or word, can be used as a general sign if we use it to denote any or all objects of a certain sort indifferently. And the proof that these general signs do not need to be formed by abstraction is that the line, which is as good an example of a general sign as any, can hardly be said to be formed in that way.

How do we go about making a word or object stand indifferently for any object of the same sort? Let us take the case of the line first, as Berkeley does. He presses the question how we know any proposition to be true of all triangles whatever, unless we have first seen it demonstrated of the abstract idea of a triangle. Suppose, for example, I demonstrate of some triangle that its angles are equal to two right angles. What tells me that my proof extends beyond this particular triangle, and is a proof in general that the angles of a triangle add up to two right angles? Berkeley replies:

To which I answer, that though the idea I have in view whilst I make the demonstration, be, for instance, that of an isosceles rectangular triangle, whose sides are of a determinate length, I may nevertheless be certain it extends to all other rectilinear triangles, of what sort or bigness soever. And that, because neither the right angle, nor the equality, nor determinate length of the sides, are at all concerned in the demonstration. (PI. 16)

Pitcher, in his excellent chapter on abstract ideas in Berkeley,[2] objects to this that for all we know the particular characteristics of the present triangle may be relevant to our proof, even though we did not explicitly mention them in our premises. The very fact that our proof was constructed on a particular triangle makes it possible that some feature not shared by all triangles was in fact relevant to the proof, and hence prevent the proof from being effective for all triangles whatever. He concludes from this that "Berkeley does not . . . satisfactorily account for the generality of geometrical demonstration" (p. 76). This seems to me to involve a confusion. For if some triangle were to turn up of which our demon-stration failed, we would simply conclude, not that the demon-stration was not general in any way, but that we had *over*generalised it. A proof of this sort is generalisable to all *relevantly similar* triangles; in this sense it is general, but our view of what makes a triangle count as relevantly similar may of course at any time be mistaken. Berkeley has given an account, consistent with the earlier passage about the line, of how a proof of a proposition for one triangle may be a proof of the same proposition for more than one, and this was really the only challenge he needed here to face.

Has Berkeley missed the point?

It may now be felt that Berkeley has missed the point. A general idea, for Locke, was one which fitted all objects of the same sort. Haven't we just said that for Berkeley a general idea only fits some objects of the sort, and that we may be in no position to say which? Whether Berkeley has missed the point depends upon what the point is. The original question was how one word can represent or stand for or name more than one object. And prior to that question, presumably, is the question of what makes it possible for a word to stand for or name anything else at all. Locke's answer to the latter question gave him his answer to the former: a word can only represent an object if it does so mediately, by being a sign for an idea which represents that object in the mind of the speaker. Locke argues for this position thus:

That then which words are the marks of are the *ideas* of the speaker; nor can anyone apply them as marks, immediately, to anything else but the *ideas* that he himself hath, for this would be to make them signs of his own conceptions and yet apply them to other *ideas*, which would be to make them signs and not signs of his *ideas* at the same time, and so in effect to have no signification at all. (*Essay* 3.2.2)

[2] Pitcher *Berkeley*, ch. 5.

This argument gives him his answer to the former question: a word can represent more than one object if the idea it immediately signifies is a general idea, and to be general an idea must perforce be abstract. And this provides the answer to yet a further question, namely what determines *which* things such a word stands for. The answer is that the word stands for anything which the abstract general idea suits.

The charge now is that Berkeley cannot provide any answer to this last question other than Locke's. To see this, let us take Berkeley's own example of the line which is used as a general sign. Which are the things which it stands for? Anything which is 'of the same sort' as itself. But what determines which things are of the same sort? Any object (including the first line) is of many sorts. What makes it the case that it stands for all lines rather than for all rectangular white patches, say? The question is which of the properties of our line are relevant to its function here as a sign. There must be some selection, and the selection at issue seems to be achieved by the intentions of the person using the sign. That person must construct in his mind a conception of the restricted group of qualities which determine the range of signification of the object he is using as a sign. The objects which count as 'of the same sort' are those which resemble the first one in those respects, other differences being irrelevant.

But if Berkeley tells some story such as this it is beginning to look more and more as if his answer doesn't differ significantly from Locke's. For surely the construction of a restricted conception of the properties held in common by all objects of the same sort is just the construction of a Lockean abstract general idea. And if Berkeley simply refuses to offer any story like this, it is clear that his position here begs the question. That question was how it is possible for one object to stand as a sign for all objects of the same sort, and Berkeley's answer simply helps itself to the central notion here, that of being 'of the same sort'. The Lockean abstract general idea determined which objects the sign signified, and Berkeley has rejected this notion and put nothing in its place.

What is Berkeley to say in reply to this? His position must be that though in a sense he does reject Locke's notion and put nothing in its place, this is really because in his view Locke's question does not need an answer, or at least not an answer of the sort that Locke offers. So the absence of an alternative answer in Berkeley is not a defect but an important part of his account. How can this be? Berkeley's position is that anything whatever can be used to stand for objects of a class, and that what explains this ability of ideas, words or other things to stand as general signs in this way is simply the fact that that is how we use them.

The first point to make, in trying to show that Berkeley's position here is substantial both in itself and in its rejection of Locke's account, is to hold that it is a mistake to think of general words as intrinsically problematic. One way to make general words seem problematic is to take as one's paradigm of a word that does make sense a proper name, a word restricted by its sense to one object. This is the way Locke approaches the matter, but it is a mistake. The temptation to which Locke succumbs is to view as the most easily understood sentence something which is as nearly as possible a list of names. But this is an unpromising starting point for the understanding of language, partly because it leads us to view with suspicion things that are not in themselves suspicious (i.e. general words), partly because it takes as unproblematic something which in fact raises the greater difficulties. Contemporary philosophy, taking it in contrast to Locke that language is inherently general, finds its difficulties in explaining how there can be words whose sense ties them to one particular object. So the matter is now reversed.

Second and more important, it is not empty to say that the aspect of our use which makes sense of the possibility of general words is the fact that we use one word, e.g. the word 'cup', as able to be true of many objects. The thrust of this statement lies in its denial of the Lockean assumption that such use needs some sort of support. It is as if we could only go on to use a word of a second object if our use of it the first time was accompanied by or generated some sort of blueprint whose nature was sufficient to stabilise and unify what would otherwise be a completely arbitrary and hence unstable practice of going on from the first case to others. The only justification for calling what we are doing 'going on in the same way' (that is to say, using the word of the second object with exactly the same sense as it had when used of the first) would be, on this approach, that each move involved an application of the *same* blueprint.

Wittgenstein has helped us to see that this approach is both unnecessary and ineffective. It is unnecessary because our practice of using the same word first of one object and then of others needs no such support. The feeling that there must be something underneath that practice to hold it up is nothing but a form of vertigo, vertigo being considered here as an unjustified fear of heights.[3] And we can see that this fear is unjustified because if it were justified it could never be put to rest. Locke's notion of an abstract general idea as a sort of blueprint in fact only raises the very problems it is designed to solve. For if there were a mystery about how to go on using the same word of different objects, it will hardly be dissipated by announcing that we can do this because they

---

[3] See L. Wittgenstein *Philosophical Investigations* (Oxford: Basil Blackwell 1968), §§ 143–242. The notion of vertigo is taken from J. McDowell 'Non-cognitivism and rule-following', in S. Holtzman and C. Leich (eds) *Wittgenstein: To Follow a Rule* (London: Routledge and Kegan Paul 1981), pp. 141–62, at p. 149.

fit the *same* blueprint. The question whether this one is really the same as the last one is as effective when asked about the blueprint as when asked about the cup. If we ask it about the blueprint, we recognise that if Locke were right we would be needing a blueprint for the blueprint, and so on *ad infinitum*. Locke's views generate an infinite regress, according to Wittgenstein.[4] And Locke concealed this from himself because he took it to be obvious that ideas are repeatable – that one can have the same one again. But in fact there is no difference between the notion of having the same idea again and having another idea of exactly the same sort. If we put on one side Locke's conviction that ideas are repeatable and that there are no problems about our ability to recognise an idea on its recurrence, the question whether this blueprint is the same as the one we used before is just the same question as the question whether the cup is the same as the one we used before – not whether it is the same one but whether it is another one of the same sort. So we conclude that if Locke were raising a proper question, it would be unanswerable. And once we recognise this, we can rest happier with Wittgenstein's claim that Locke's question represents a hopeless search for a solid basis for an ability that does not need it, and that we must simply learn to live with the feeling of vertigo. The seeming need for the reassurance of that basis is an intellectual disease, from which Wittgenstein's arguments are intended to cure us.

I have expressed this Wittgensteinian defence of Berkeley as revolving around the notion of 'going on in the same way'. But the same point can be made about the ability of a proof to count as a proof for all lines rather than just for the line on which the proof was done. There is nothing in the original process that determines which other objects the proof is a proof for, and Locke was wrong to insist that our procedure here makes no sense in the absence of a blueprint to serve this purpose. That the proof is a general proof is determined by the way we use it, and how general it is is not fixed by any aspect of the original proof or of the user's intentions. Such matters are left undetermined, without this meaning that there is no such thing as general thought, general signification or general proof.[5]

Some philosophers take the view that Berkeley is not offering the account of generality that I have just outlined, but is in essential agreement with Locke. The only reason for doubting this, according to J.L. Mackie, derives from a misreading of Locke.[6] We understood Locke

[4] See *Philosophical Investigations*, §§ 85–7.
[5] For a helpful introduction to such thoughts about proofs, see I. Lakatos *Proofs And Refutations*, edited by J. Worrall and E. Zahar (Cambridge: Cambridge University Press 1976), ch. 1.
[6] J. L. Mackie *Problems from Locke* (Oxford: Oxford University Press 1976), ch. 4.

to be saying that in abstraction we create from many similar ideas an entirely new idea, shorn of such considerations as would bind it and do bind them to some particular object. Mackie suggests that this is not what Locke is saying, taking as his main evidence the passage quoted earlier in this chapter:

And *thus they come to have a general name*, and a general *idea*. Wherein they make nothing new, but only leave out of the complex *idea* they had of *Peter* and *James*, *Mary* and *Jane* that which is peculiar to each, and retain only what is common to them all.

Mackie argues that Locke's doctrine is one of *selective attention* to a restricted group of qualities of an already existing idea, rather than the creation of an entirely new abstract general idea. Any particular idea (that of Peter, say) can serve as an abstract general idea, if we attend only to those elements of it in respect of which Peter does not differ from other objects of the same sort. If we approach the matter in this way, we are not in the business of constructing the sort of abstract ideas to which Berkeley took such exception, namely ideas of objects having determinable but not determinate qualities. For all the ideas we entertain are ideas of objects enjoying a full complement of determinate qualities; it is only that we don't pay any attention to those aspects of the ideas in using them as general, i.e. to stand for all objects of the same sort.

Berkeley's position, according to Mackie, is essentially the same. In using a word, idea or object to stand for all objects of the same sort, we are using things which clearly have properties other than those relevant to the purpose; we can distinguish between relevant and irrelevant properties of our *archetype*, and use the original object to stand indifferently for all those which share with it the relevant ones, leaving differences in respect of the irrelevant ones out of account.

There are three ways in which this compromise fails. First, I do not agree that the theory of abstraction as selective attention can reasonably be attributed to Locke, and this means that if, as I shall argue, it was not Berkeley's either, it ends up being held by neither rather than by both as Mackie claims. In my view, the phrase quoted above, "Wherein they make nothing new", should be held to mean only that they add nothing beyond what experience has already provided, but only take away some elements, leaving what is essentially a new idea. Second, Berkeley does not agree with Locke that generality is achieved by selective attention to an idea. His view, as we have seen, is that no idea is needed to stand as intermediary between word and objects for the word to be able to denote more than one object indifferently. Part of what is being rejected here is the Lockean insistence that representation is a matter of resemblance between idea and object; for the general word is held able to represent many objects directly, without for that reason needing to resemble them in any respect at all. Third, however, and more important, is the fact that the doctrine of abstraction as selective attention renders it unfit to perform one crucial task, namely that of showing how we can achieve the absolute conception of the world. For the purposes of that conception, it is insufficient simply to concentrate one's attention on certain selected features of the world, and then announce that one has thereby achieved a conception of a world which has only those features. As we said earlier, the realist has not merely to achieve the negative conception of a world which he is only considering as having certain properties, but the positive conception of a world which he is considering as having only certain properties. This is a much more demanding matter, and one which Mackie's view of abstraction as selective attention does not serve. I think that we have no alternative than to attribute to Locke the full-blooded theory of abstraction to which Berkeley takes reasonable exception.

Does the realist attempt an illegitimate abstraction?

Berkeley makes the forceful claim that realism is a doctrine caused by a mistaken operation of Locke's notion of abstraction. He writes:

For can there be a nicer strain of abstraction than to distinguish the existence of sensible objects from their being perceived, so as to conceive them existing unperceived? . . . Hence as it is impossible for me to see or feel any thing without an actual sensation of that thing, so is it impossible for me to conceive in my thoughts any sensible thing or object distinct from the sensation or perception of it. (P. 5)

What is the idea here? We can reasonably expect that Berkeley takes his discussion of abstraction in the Introduction to have exposed the mistake with which he is here charging the realist. Now at PI. 6 Berkeley suggests that an interest in the abuse of language leads him to take notice

of what seems to have had a chief part in rendering speculation intricate and perplexed, and to have occasioned innumerable errors and difficulties in almost all parts of knowledge. And that is the opinion that the mind hath a power of framing *abstract ideas* or notions of things. He who is not a perfect stranger to the writings and disputes of philosophers, must needs acknowledge that no small part of them are spent about abstract ideas. These are in a more especial manner, thought to be the object of those sciences which go by the name of *logic* and *metaphysics*

The abstract ideas of which Berkeley seems to be speaking here are, to judge by the succeeding examples (PI. 7), those of motion, extension (shape) and colour. Berkeley could therefore be saying simply that these notions are dubious or insecure just because they have been formed by abstraction. But this by itself doesn't show why these notions are more dubious than other general notions, the ones which are not peculiar to logic and metaphysics; nor does it show why the fact that they have been formed by abstraction lends them particularly to the generation of the error in realism. I think that Berkeley holds that the realist's conception of physical objects as able to exist independent of perceiving minds, and the use of the primary/secondary distinction to say that there is available to us an absolute conception of the world as it exists out of all relation to minds, both depend upon a use of the operation of abstraction that is illegitimate in the way he claims to have exposed. How does this work?

At the end of the last chapter we argued against Berkeley's claim in the First Dialogue that to say that one conceives something existing unconceived is as much a contradiction as to say that one sees something existing unseen. We held that this claim was at once irrelevant and false. It was irrelevant because the realist could and should say that all he needs to do is to conceive of something that is *able* to exist unconceived, not which does in fact do so. It was false because to say that one conceives of something existing unconceived is not to say that one conceives of something that does in fact exist unconceived, but only to say that one conceives of something *as* existing unconceived. But now we can begin to see that Berkeley's real point is not, as he there claimed, that the realist's position involves a simple contradiction. Rather he is suggesting that the attempt to conceive of something *as* existing unconceived is as misguided as the attempt to conceive of a man *as* having no particular colour or height, and similarly that the attempt to conceive of something *able* to exist unconceived is no better than the attempt to conceive of a man *able* to have no particular colour or height. All involve impossible feats of abstraction.

Abstraction is subtraction; an abstract idea is formed by subtracting some elements from ideas furnished by experience, leaving in acceptable cases an idea of something which could still exist as we now conceive it. Berkeley's claim, and his central insight, is that in holding that we can conceive of things capable of existing unconceived we are holding that we can subtract from the content of an idea every aspect that concerns its relation to the mind and leave as residue a conception of something sufficiently rich to be capable of independent existence. But we cannot subtract from the content of an idea of ours every aspect that concerns its relation to the mind, without leaving an incomplete conception. Our attempt would be exactly like that of conceiving of a pain as able to exist

out of all relation to the mind (unperceived, at least); we cannot d
because if we subtract from our idea of pain the element of its
presented to a mind, we end up with an idea of something which could
not exist. We cannot, then, start off from something essentially mental,
be it pain or idea, extract from its content every mental aspect, and
announce that we have achieved a conception of something capable of
the realist's independent existence.

It is no reply to suggest that we can achieve a conception of an object
capable of such existence by simply leaving out of our idea any reference
to a relation to a perceiving mind. We came across this suggestion before
in the case of conceiving of an object without conceiving of its colour,
and it is no better this time round. This negative approach would, in the
case of pain, be to conceive of a pain without conceiving of somebody
having it. But even if Berkeley would allow this as a possibility, which I
doubt, the real point is that the realist has to do more than this if he is to
achieve what he is really after, namely a positive conception of an object
as existing or as capable of existing out of all relation to the mind; which
in the case of pain would be a positive conception of a pain which is
hurting nobody. The absurdity lies in the attempt to strip off from
something essentially mental every mental aspect and then suppose that
something substantial remains.

So Berkeley is arguing that if we are restricted to starting from our
ideas and then attempt to move from them to achieve a conception of
something like an idea but which can survive the loss of all relation to the
mind, we shall never succeed. And the realist cannot escape this by
choosing another starting point, for this starting point, as we saw at the
beginning of the last chapter, is definitive of empiricism, which is
common to both Locke and Berkeley. Berkeley's point is then that
empiricism and realism are incompatible. The only consistent way of
being an empiricist is to join him as an idealist, for if we are to start from
experience (ideas) we can never move beyond it to a conception of
something to which the possibility of being experienced is merely
accidental.

The conclusion that empiricism and realism are incompatible is
perhaps the main conclusion of the *Principles*, though we have expressed
it in terms that Berkeley would not have used. It is his central insight,
which the last two chapters have seen him groping towards in various
ways.

The same thoughts that demolish the realist's pretensions also destroy
the primary/secondary distinction and the possibility of the absolute
conception of the world. First, if realism is impossible, Locke cannot
hold his preferentially realist attitude towards the primary qualities. But,
more importantly, that attitude engenders acceptance that there is such a

thing as the absolute conception, and this is what Berkeley is really against. For it amounts to the general supposition that our experience of the world is non-essential to it. In Berkeley's view, this is an, or rather *the*, impossible feat of abstraction.

Finally, we can see in Berkeley's denial of the possibility of abstraction the real reason why he holds that an idea can resemble nothing but an idea. In conceiving of the realist's independent world we are supposing that there are objects like our ideas but shorn of all relation to a mind. But we can form no conception of any such object except by illegitimate use of abstraction. Contrary to what that use would require, the relation to a mind is essential to any possible object of the mind. Our minds cannot have as their objects anything to which relation to mind is merely accidental, and so our ideas can resemble nothing but other ideas. This is the last layer of that by now familiar doctrine.

In chapter 2 I suggested that Berkeley made two promising attacks on realism, which were apparently independent. The first was based on the claim that an idea can resemble nothing but an idea, and the second revolved around the notion of abstraction. It now emerges that the first of these depends in the end upon the second, and that Berkeley's rejection of realism does have a unity greater than his own text would suggest. This is, I think, an advantage. It is always better in philosophy to have one sound position rather than several dodgy ones, just as (in an analogy which I owe to A. G. N. Flew) it is better to have one good bucket than ten leaky ones.

In this chapter we have been attempting to identify Berkeley's main argument against realism, and to see how it fits with the many other considerations with which he surrounds it. In taking the central argument to be that the realist attempts an impossible abstraction, we have not only taken Berkeley at his word, but also made the best sense of the otherwise odd fact that the Introduction to the *Principles* seems to be entirely about language, in a way which is hardly taken up afterwards and whose relevance may therefore seem rather obscure. And we have revealed a unity in Berkeley's thought which is itself a strength.

4
God

In previous chapters we have examined Berkeley's arguments against Locke's realism. Now we turn to Berkeley's own account of the world, his idealism. That account should and does emerge from the perceived defects of realism. The world, for us, can only consist of elements of which we can conceive. We can only conceive of ideas. Therefore the world we conceive of must consist only of ideas. This tells us the nature of the material world. Instead of being a Lockean world of microscopic particles with only primary qualities, held together in suspension in a way of which we cannot conceive, it is a world of ideas, a world that is not capable of existing out of all relations to minds.

For Locke, qualities cannot exist independently; a quality needs an object to belong to, to be the quality of. Similarly, for Berkeley, ideas cannot exist independently; they depend for their existence on there being minds to have them. For an idea to exist it must exist in some mind. The material world, which consists entirely of ideas, must if it is to exist at all exist in some mind or minds. There are two sorts of things in Berkeley's world, then: minds, and their ideas. And there are no other sorts of things in it. These are all the sorts of things that there are.

Responses to Berkeley varied and still vary from scornful rejection, through intrigued amusement, to enthusiastic acceptance. In his own time Dean Swift is said to have instructed his servant not to bother to open the door to Berkeley when he knocked, on the uncomprehending view that on his own principles Berkeley should be able to walk straight through it. And when asked his opinion of Berkeley's philosophy, Dr Johnson simply kicked a large stone, saying "I refute it *thus*". (This is probably even worse than Johnson's response to the problem of the freedom of the will: "Sir, we *know* our will is free, and *there's* an end on't".) I shall try to show that enthusiasm, if not acceptance, is the most suitable response.

The simplicity of Berkeley's system is such that he only needs the first thirty-three paragraphs of the *Principles* to give its general outline. At that point (P. 34) he begins to consider and rebut various more or less effective objections. But the last sections of *Principles* 1–33 contain his reply to the most serious and central objection of all. Surely a world that consists entirely of ideas is a world from which all reality has been expunged. How can there be room for real tables and chairs in Berkeley's world? An imaginary table seems to have the same status as a real one, on Berkeley's account. He puts the point thus:

First then, it will be objected that by the foregoing principles, all that is real and substantial in nature is banished out of the world: . . . All things that exist, exist only in the mind, that is, they are purely notional. What therefore becomes of the sun, moon, and stars? . . . I answer, that by the principles premised, we are not deprived of any one thing in nature. Whatever we see, feel, hear, or any wise conceive or understand, remains as secure as ever, and is as real as ever. There is a *rerum natura*, and the distinction between realities and chimeras retains its full force. (P. 34)

Berkeley's position is that though everything is idea, some ideas are the real things, and others are the merely imaginary ones. What is the difference between them? He answers:

The ideas imprinted on the senses by the author of nature are called real things: and those excited in the imagination being less regular, vivid and constant, are more properly termed *ideas*, or *images of things*, which they copy and represent. But then our sensations, be they never so vivid and distinct, are nevertheless *ideas*, that is, they exist in the mind, or are perceived by it, as truly as the ideas of its own framing. (P. 33)

So the ideas caused in us by God are the real things, and the ones we make up for ourselves are the imaginary ones. Our awareness of the ideas that are real could be more properly termed perception; our awareness of the others is imagination.

Berkeley wants to persuade us that his system leaves the reality of the material world untouched, the only difference being that we are not used to thinking of the real world as consisting entirely of ideas:

But, say you, it sounds very harsh to say we eat and drink ideas, and are clothed with ideas. I acknowledge it does so, the word *idea* not being used in common discourse to signify the several combinations of sensible qualities, which are called *things*: and it is certain that any expression which varies from the familiar use of language, will seem harsh and ridiculous. But this does not concern the truth of the proposition, which in other words is no more than to say, we are fed and clothed with those things which we perceive immediately by our senses. (P. 38)

We shall inquire at the beginning of the next chapter whether Berkeley does in fact preserve the common distinction between the real and the imaginary as well as he protests. Here we pursue a different path. Berkeley's method of preserving that distinction depends entirely upon the success of a move we have not so far considered, namely his proof of the existence of God. For if that proof fails Berkeley loses with it his positive account of the reality of the material world. And Berkeley is particularly proud of the ability of his system to provide a proof of God's existence. As the title page of the *Principles* indicates, he thinks that realism is one of the chief causes of atheism, for it leaves us with a conception of a world to which the existence of God is a comparative irrelevance. In Berkeley's eyes, one of the strengths of idealism is the central place it gives to God.

We will see further aspects of this centrality as we go along. For the moment the question is how to generate a proof of God on idealist premises. The normal view, derived from Jonathan Bennett, is that there are two such proofs or arguments; the first can be called the independence argument (Bennett calls it the passivity argument), and the second the continuity argument.[1]

The independence argument occurs first at *Principles* 29, but it depends upon a result established at sections 25–6. Every idea that occurs in a mind must be caused by something. But no idea can be the cause of anything, for ideas are wholly passive and a cause is necessarily something that acts. The only things, therefore, that can cause ideas are minds, which are active, as we know from the ability of our imagination to create ideas. The ideas which we don't cause must therefore be caused by some other mind. So far this would leave it open that the ideas which we don't cause (what Berkeley calls the ideas of sense) are caused by several contributing minds, none of which is particularly special. But according to Berkeley the nature of the ideas of sense provides us with compelling reason to suppose first that the ideas of sense are all caused by the same mind, and second that that mind enjoys remarkable powers. First, we can suppose that if there were several minds involved, some trace of the differences between them would emerge in their effects. But a remarkable feature of the world of sense is its consistency. We do in general require that every truth be consistent with every other truth, and we are able to do this because reality is internally consistent. For that very reason it does not reveal traces of the working of more than one mind; every realist must agree with Berkeley's contention that, within his system, this is so. But now we can begin to attribute to that one mind the qualities necessary for the production of the ideas of sense, and these

---

[1] See J. Bennett *Locke, Berkeley, Hume: Central Themes* (Oxford: Oxford University Press 1971), ch. 7. Bennett's version of the independence argument differs slightly from mine.

qualities begin to mount gradually until we are attributing to that mind the traditional properties of the Christian God. As Berkeley says in the Second Dialogue:

And from the variety, order, and manner of these, I conclude the author of them to be *wise, powerful, and good, beyond comprehension.* (p. 215)

First, it is a mind of unimaginable power, since it creates and sustains all the ideas of sense. Every detail of the world we see around us adds to the power we must attribute to that mind; the incredible combination of complexity and consistency is all the evidence we could need. Second, it is a benevolent mind, since the very order we see in the world argues the care that mind is taking to enable us to run our lives in some safety. The regularity betrayed by the ideas of sense is what we rely on to better our lot, both in ordinary practical terms and in theoretical science. So the nature of the ideas of sense provides us with overwhelming evidence that there is a unique, omnipotent and benevolent mind causing those ideas in us. This is the independence argument.

The continuity argument is quite different. The simplest version starts from the premise that the things we see continue to exist when we cease to see them. But the things we see are ideas, and ideas cannot exist except in some mind. There must therefore be some other mind wherein they exist during the gaps in our awareness of them.

This is a remarkable argument for Berkeley to use, if only because it does not seem as if he has the right to help himself to the first premise. One suggestion is that he thinks himself justified in adopting this premise because it is a matter of common sense. But Berkeley's willingness to accept the dictates of common sense is rather selective, and needs to be assessed case by case. In this instance it is hard to imagine why he thinks it must be true that the things we see, which on his own showing are only ideas, should persist when we cease to see them. Surely his first thought should be to question the necessary continuity of the things we see, rather than to accept it unquestioningly as the basis for a proof of the existence of God. Indeed, the continuity of material objects is something that on any account needs to be argued for, and one might think that if it brings with it a proof of God's existence we should have to argue all the harder for it rather than allow ourselves to take it for granted.

It also seems that the continuity of material objects is, for Berkeley, something which could only be established *after* God's existence is proved. It may be true that such continuity is only possible if God exists, but this provides no justification for taking continuity for granted and proving God's existence from it. This route would be dangerous; it would be like arguing from:

There are real things, and
Real things continue to exist when we are not aware of them

to

There must be a mind that perceives them when we do not.

This would be manifestly circular as a Berkeleian proof of God because
the first premise, as we have shown, depends upon an antecedent proof
of God. The continuity argument can therefore only be some form of
supplementary to the main argument, the independence argument.

   This, at least, is the standard view, offered by Bennett. Bennett argues
forcefully that though Berkeley sometimes seems to use the continuity
argument, it is not available to him; and he is only seduced into using it
by a mistake into which he falls because of an ambiguity in the notion of
independence.

   In the light of the preceding comments, we should be cautious before
admitting that Berkeley does in fact use the continuity argument at all.
Bennett cites some passages where Berkeley does seem to wield
considerations of continuity. The most striking is in the Third Dialogue:

Now it is plain they have an existence exterior to my mind, since I find them by
experience to be independent of it. There is therefore some other mind wherein
they exist, during the intervals between the times of my perceiving them: as
likewise they did before my birth, and would do after my supposed annihilation.
(pp. 230–1)

There is a passage in the Second Dialogue whose general tenor is more
dubious:

. . . sensible things cannot exist otherwise than in a mind or spirit. Whence I
conclude, not that they have no real existence, but that seeing they depend not
on my thought, and have an existence distinct from being perceived by me, *there
must be some other mind wherein they exist.* . . . I immediately and necessarily
conclude the being of a God, because all sensible things must be perceived by
him. (p. 212)

Is this the independence argument, an argument entirely free from
thoughts of continuity? Berkeley here argues that the ideas of sense,
which are independent of me and have a distinct existence (we shall have
to ask later what this means) must exist in some other mind as well as in
mine. This is a position beyond anything contained in the independence
argument, which held merely that there must be another mind to cause

the ideas of sense, not to have them or perceive them as well. And the point here is that once we have admitted that we have reason, from the very nature of the ideas of sense, to believe that they exist in some other mind as well as in ours, we are moving towards a position in which we attribute to those ideas a continuous as well as an independent existence.

The suggestion I am exploring, then, is that thoughts of continuity and thoughts of independence are not as separate as Bennett suggests. Relevant here is a passage which Bennett cites to show that Berkeley's grasp on the central notion of independence is not very secure. Berkeley uses that notion in a diagnosis of the errors of realism:

men knowing they perceived several ideas, whereof they themselves were not the authors, as not being excited from within, nor depending on the operation of their wills, this made them maintain, those ideas or objects of perception had an existence independent of, and without the mind, without ever dreaming that a contradiction was involved in those words. (P. 56)

Berkeley is here discerning two senses of 'independent'. In the first, 'independent of' means 'not caused by'; the ideas of sense are independent of our minds in this sense. In the second, 'independent of' means 'not owned by'. In this sense too our ideas of sense have an existence independent of our minds. But Berkeley is insisting here that it is a simple mistake to conclude from this that the ideas of sense have an existence independent of, i.e. unowned by any mind whatever. This is the realist's mistake, and it involves the contradiction of which the realist is guilty.

What Berkeley is not saying here is that it is a fallacy to argue from one sense of 'independent' to the other. The realist's error was to move from 'unowned by my mind' to 'unowned by any mind'. Berkeley thinks that though the two senses are distinct, we *can* move from one to the other, as the Second Dialogue passage makes clear:

seeing they depend not on my thought, . . . there must be some other mind wherein they exist.

This is to say that an idea cannot be caused in my mind by a mind in which that idea does not exist. This is only common sense, for how could the causing mind know what it was doing unless it knew which idea it was causing in my mind? And how could it know what idea it was causing unless that idea was present to it, that is to say, in it? Bennett would want to say, of course, that this does not get us to a fully-fledged continuity argument, since that argument requires us to have reason to attribute to the ideas of sense a continuous existence throughout the gaps in our perception of them. But this point is only effective against an interpretation of Berkeley as putting forward two independent arguments for the existence of God; it has no effect against someone who holds that for Berkeley continuity and independence go together.

Bennett, it emerges, has two views. The first is that Berkeley does not in fact use the continuity argument, despite the existing consensus of opinion that he does. With this I agree, if the continuity argument is to be thought of as an argument separate from the independence argument. But the second view is that Berkeley is really not interested in considerations of continuity at all. This seems to me to be false; according to me, Berkeley took it that considerations of independence and continuity cannot be disentangled, and are all part of one argument. If this is true, Berkeley agrees here with Hume's assertion that there are logical links between the (ownership) claim that the objects of sense are continuous and the (causal) claim that they are independent. Hume holds that though questions of independence and of continuity are separate, they are tightly interconnected:

> We ought to examine apart those two questions, which are commonly confounded together, *viz.* Why we attribute a CONTINU'D existence to objects, even when we suppose they are not present to the senses; and why we suppose them to have an existence DISTINCT from the mind and perception. Under this last head I comprehend their situation as well as relations, their *external* position as well as the *independence* of their existence and operation. These two questions concerning the continu'd and distinct existence of body are intimately connected together. For if the objects of our senses continue to exist, even when they are not perceiv'd, their existence is of course independent of and distinct from the perception; and *vice versa*, if their existence be independent of the perception and distinct from it, they must continue to exist, even tho' they be not perceiv'd . . . the decision of one question decides the other.[2]

It has been a critical commonplace to say that Hume is wrong on this last point. H. H. Price remarks:

> This . . . does not strictly follow. It is conceivable that even so they might still have an interrupted being. Only, the interruptions in their being would not then be due to interruptions in our observations of them.[3]

More recent discussions of the nature of objectivity, however, have tended to suggest that the continuity of objects is as important for their

---

[2] D. Hume *A Treatise of Human Nature*, edited by L. A. Selby-Bigge and revised by P. Nidditch (Oxford: Clarendon Press 1978), bk. 1, pt. 4, sec. 2, at p. 188.

[3] H. H. Price *Hume's Theory of the External World* (Oxford: Oxford University Press 1940), p. 18.

status as objective constituents of the world as is their independence.[4] And if this were true, Berkeley has a choice. Either, as Bennett suggests, he is not interested in continuity, in which case he fails to assimilate within his idealist picture of the world one feature critical to the objectivity we ascribe to that world. Or he recognises (albeit dimly) the importance attached to continuity as an element central to our view of the world as objective, and expresses that importance by seeing the independence argument as also concerned with continuity. I am suggesting that Berkeley took, and was right to take, the latter course.

Why would it be right to see continuity as an essential element in objectivity? The crucial idea here is the need to be able to think of the things we see as recurring, or at least as able to recur; we need to be able to reidentify objects and to distinguish between the reappearance of an old object and the appearance of a new one indistinguishable from the first. Only in this way can we begin to plot our way around the world and to conceive of ourselves as moving from place to place. Places can only exist if there is continuity, for only then can we make sense of the difference between returning to the same place and reaching a new one which we cannot distinguish from the first. If continuity has this sort of critical importance in constructing the notion of an objective spatial world within which we are operating, Berkeley is right to care deeply about the need to make sense of the world as existing continuously. For only in that way could he reasonably claim that "Whatever we see, feel, or any wise conceive or understand, remains as secure as ever, and is as real as ever" (P. 34).

It is not just that the ordinary man believes and is right to believe that the world we experience is continuous; and that therefore Berkeley reasonably finds room within his system for such a thought. The suggestion is instead that we experience the world as spatial, and that such experience is incoherent if the world is not continuous. On pain of distorting our experience, then, we are constrained to think of our world as continuous. It is not a far cry from this to say that we experience the world as continuous.

It is not required for this purpose, of course, that every object (idea of sense) be conceived of as existing in perpetuity. We all know that most objects had a beginning and will have an end, probably before we see them again. But it is required, if we are to think of an idea as recurring to us, that we conceive of it as having existed all the while. That is to say that Berkeley is right to hold that if there are intervals between our

[4] See P. F. Strawson *Individuals: An Essay in Descriptive Metaphysics* (London: Methuen 1959), ch. 2; and G. Evans 'Things without the mind', in Z. van Straaten (ed.) *Philosophical Subjects* (Oxford: Clarendon Press 1980), pp. 76–116.

perceptions of an object, we must take that object to have a continuous existence during the intervals. To the extent that it is important for the realist to insist on the persistence of such objects and places as are to be reidentified or rediscovered, to that extent Berkeley is justified in arguing that this is only possible if there is a continuously existing God to make sense of the persistence.

The position, then, is not that every idea of sense must persist both before and after our perception of it, and that we know this because we have somehow inferred it from the independence of the ideas of sense. All that the independence tells us is that those ideas exist in some other mind as well as in our own, not for how long they must exist there. The need for continuity derives from the need to give a sense within Berkeley's system to the idea that the world we live in is a spatial world within which we navigate; those places which we visit and revisit, and their occupants, must count as continuing occupants of space. And for this to be possible there must be a continuous perceiver, since we know that the continuance of our objects, though it requires the continuing existence of some mind, is not guaranteed by the continuous awareness of human minds like ours.

The role of God in Berkeley's system

At the beginning of this chapter we noticed that Berkeley intended his idealist system to have the desirable consequence of showing how central a place God has in our world. In his opinion, Locke's mechanistic world was like a large clock, which only needed a God to wind it up. Once God had been kind enough to wind it, his role in affairs was finished; the world had no more need of him, and could get along perfectly well on its own. This was in contrast to the way Descartes conceived of things. For Descartes, the world needed God in order to keep going; God's role is distinguished from that of an ordinary parent just on the grounds that parents are not needed to sustain their offspring (at least not for long) while God is needed to sustain the world as well as to start it up.[5]

Berkeley agreed with Descartes here (and on other matters) rather than with Locke, though of course he took the matter from his idealist point of view. The world we live in is just the passing show of ideas that are the real things. Something is necessary to keep this passing show on the road, as the independence argument for the existence of God

[5] See the third of Descartes' *Meditations on First Philosophy*, in *Descartes: Philosophical Writings*, edited by E. Anscombe and P. T. Geach (London: Nelson 1954), at p. 88.

showed; that thing must be a mind of a power greater than any we can conceive. But there is a difference between Descartes' realist approach to this matter and Berkeley's idealist one. A realist like Descartes is at liberty to hold that God's continuing activity is required for the continuity of the world. But the need for God here is a causal need. God is an outsider, a sort of addition to the world, not an essential part of it. It is not an internal requirement of that world that God should exist to support its continuity, but an external requirement stemming from external considerations. God is not metaphysically necessary to it, but only causally necessary. For Berkeley, by contrast, the need for a continuing God is internal to his conception of the world. It follows directly from the nature of the world as idea.

Of course it is not just for the continuity of the comparatively few things we see that God is required as a persisting mind. He is required for the even more demanding job of keeping the whole sensible world going:

As sure therefore as the sensible world really exists, so sure is there an infinite omnipresent Spirit who contains and supports it. ... I immediately and necessarily conclude the being of a God, because all sensible things must be perceived by him. (Second Dialogue, p. 212)

So the idea that there should be a world, and not just a random distribution of a few persisting objects, requires us to think of God as permanently aware of every part of it.

But God's existence and presence is even more central to Berkeley's world than this. So far we have accepted Berkeley's argument that *our* ideas need a cause, and that that cause must be a mind not very like ours. But this would leave God very much in the position of being the conclusion of an argument, not as a person with whom we are in intimate and continuous contact. Berkeley in fact brings God far closer than the independence argument initially suggests, by maintaining that the ideas which are the real things are not just ideas which God caused in us, but ideas in the mind of God. On this view, the world we live in, *our* world, is nothing other than (part of) the contents of the mind of God. It is not just that God causes us to have ideas *like* his; when we open our eyes and see what is there, we are having ideas which are God's.

It is not always clear that this is Berkeley's view. The position expounded in the *Principles* is nearer to the simpler, Bennett version of the independence argument; and even in the *Three Dialogues* he is not consistent in preferring the more sophisticated version that I have been imputing to him. He sometimes works with a distinction between an idea and its *archetype*, which he finds in Locke. For Locke, many of our ideas, particularly those of material objects and of species of animals and plants, are derived from real things or properties which we have encountered in the world. The ideas are, as it were, designed to fit their archetypes; fitting in this case may be expressed either in terms of resemblance or in terms of a causal relation, but resemblance is obviously the central notion despite Locke's doctrine that ideas of secondary qualities do not resemble their archetypes. Now Berkeley also is willing to talk in terms of archetypes, and as soon as he does so it becomes possible that he is flirting with the thought that the archetypes of our ideas are ideas in the mind of God. If this were so, our ideas would not be identical with God's ideas, since there is no sense in holding that ideas are identical with their archetypes; we might as well drop the distinction between idea and archetype altogether. But in fact Berkeley is very cagey in his talk of archetypes, and never commits himself explicitly to the view that God's ideas are archetypes of our own; his explicit remarks are all in the other direction. We have already seen the passage from the Third Dialogue:

it is plain [sensible things] have an existence exterior to my mind, since I find them by experience to be independent of it. There is therefore some other mind wherein they exist, during the intervals between the times of my perceiving them: (pp. 230–1)

Here Berkeley asserts explicitly that the ideas of real things exist in the mind of God. It is true that he seems to talk rather of the intervals when we are not perceiving them than of the times when they are in our minds. But that makes no real difference, for he is hardly going to maintain that the ideas that God causes us to see are transferred from his mind to ours, leaving God presumably thinking of other things. The one passage where Berkeley talks explicitly of archetypes existing in the mind of God does not in fact support the view that the real things are ideas which are not God's but ours. In this passage Berkeley is defending himself against the objection that his idealism can make no sense of the Biblical account of the Creation. The problem arises because that account held that God brought the material world into existence *before* he created any minds other than his own to perceive it. The question was exactly what happened when the material world began to exist. Berkeley could not say that God created some new ideas, because this would imply some change in the mind of God, who is unchanging. But what else could have happened? Berkeley tries the suggestion that God caused the material world to begin to exist in causing angels to perceive it, but this line is not very convincing. He then resorts to a rhetorical question:

Do I not acknowledge a twofold state of things, the one ectypal or natural, the

other archetypal and eternal? The former was created in time; the latter existed
from everlasting in the mind of God. (Third Dialogue, p. 254)

It looks as if Berkeley is going to say that the archetypal and eternal are
the ideas in the mind of God, and the 'ectypal' and natural are the real
things existing in our minds. But this wouldn't fit the purpose of the
discussion at this point. Berkeley is trying to render his account
compatible with the doctrine of the Creation, and for that purpose it
would be worse than useless to distinguish between archetypes existing
in God's mind and ectypes existing in created (i.e. our) minds. The
ectypes have to exist where the archetypes do, since at this moment in the
creation there is only one mind around (not counting the angels, whom
we have agreed to be irrelevant), and that is God. So this passage affords
no help to the claim that Berkeley eventually concluded that the ideas
which are real things are copies in our minds of ideas in the mind of God.

It is, of course, another question whether he ought to have adopted
this position. Two sorts of considerations are relevant here. The first is
whether his general position would have been improved by this altera-
tion. The second is whether it is not in fact obviously false to say that an
idea can exist in more than one mind at once. I think, first, that there are
good reasons from within Berkeley's position why he should stick to the
view that our ideas of real things are identical with ideas in the mind of
God, and, second, that this 'better' position is not obviously false.

There are two sorts of reasons why Berkeley should hold that in
perception God causes us to have ideas that are at the same time in his
mind. First is his stress on the fact that we experience the ideas of sense
as independent of us and therefore as distinct from us. This is only
possible if they exist in some other mind than our own. Thus in the
Second Dialogue we have:

seeing they depend not on my thought, and have an existence distinct from being
perceived by me, *there must be some other mind wherein they exist.* (p. 212).

and in the Third Dialogue:

Now it is plain they have an existence exterior to my mind, since I find them by
experience to be independent of it. (p. 230)

Berkeley's argument for the existence of God (and now I allow myself
to speak in the singular) is an argument from the objectivity of the
experienced world. There are various facets to that objectivity. One is the
continuity, or at least the possible continuity, of the objects of perception.
Another is the availability of the distinction between the perceptual state

and the object of that state. There are two aspects to this distinction, brought out by Hume when he spoke of "their *external* position as well as the *independence* of their operation". It has been regrettably common for commentators to be a bit rude about the notion of externality Hume is employing here, asking what the perceived world is being supposed to be external to.[6] The question they are after is whether the world is thought of as external to our bodies (which raises the question whether we can perceive our own bodies) or as external to our minds (which introduces an unsteady distinction between what is internal and what is external to the mind). Actually I think that Hume's notion makes quite good sense. The distinction is between inner and outer experience. Inner experience, as in the case of sensations, presents itself as an awareness of something which has no existence independent of our awareness of it. Outer experience, of which the paradigm instance is perception, presents itself as the awareness of something which is out there for us to be aware of. Berkeley wants to accept and recognise this distinction in his own terms. But the only sense he can give to the externality of perception is the claim that an idea of sense (that is, outer sense) must have an existence in a mind other than that mind for which it is outer. And Berkeley does make just this claim, for which reason he has to take the view that for God there is no such thing as perception. The ideas which for us are the ideas of perception are for God ideas of the imagination; ideas, that is to say, of an inner rather than of an outer sense. Berkeley takes this line because otherwise the independence argument would apply all over again to the ideas in God's mind, causing an infinite regress of independence arguments and a consequently infinite number of Gods.

The second sort of reason for Berkeley to hold that in perception we become aware of ideas in the mind of God lies in the second sort of reason he had for believing in the existence of God. This was that only if there were a permanent mind perceiving all the ideas that make up the material world would we be able to think of the world in spatial terms. For spatial distinctions rely upon the possibility of reidentification and of there being two different but indistinguishable places. And these possibilities only exist, for Berkeley, if there is a single persisting awareness into which we as passing observers are keyed.

There are two ways of taking this sort of argument for God, and it is important to see that Berkeley's way is the stronger. He could argue, weakly, that the realist wants to think in terms of reidentifiable particulars and numerically different but indistinguishable places, and that the idealist can offer this sort of thought, but only if there is a God as the

---

[6] See (e.g.) Price *Hume's Theory of the External World*, p. 19.

necessary sort of persisting awareness. This is a weak argument, and uncharacteristic of Berkeley. The general style of Berkeleian arguments for God is that we distort our experience if we deny that there is a God. So what Berkeley should be doing is to argue that our experience presents itself in spatial terms; since we experience the world as spatial, there must be the sort of persisting mind without which that kind of experience is impossible, and the persistence at issue is in a sense represented to us in our experience. And the reason why there must be this sort of mind is that the only other possible ground for the possibility of reidentifiable particulars and similar spaces would be the existence of Lockean physical objects, which have already been ruled out.

Why is this a reason for holding that our ideas of (outer) sense must be identical with, rather than mere copies of, ideas in the mind of God? We might think that the possibility of having the same idea again is served as well by the existence in the mind of God of permanent ideas of which our ideas are fleeting copies, as by the more extreme claim that those permanent ideas are occasionally present in our minds as well. I find this thought unconvincing. Let us suppose that there are two indistinguishable places in the world. What would be the difference, for someone who has visited one, between returning to it and going for the first time to the other? As far as he is concerned, there might be no difference that he could tell. But would there *be* a difference? For there to be two such places, God presumably must have two indistinguishable ideas. (This is difficult enough, but it is the same for both theories.) If we suppose ourselves returning to the first place, we must suppose that God is causing in us an idea like one of those ideas rather than the other. But this would make no sense, for if God's two ideas are indistinguishable any idea of ours that is like one of them is equally like the other. Shall we suppose instead that God is *intending* to cause in us an idea like one of his rather than the other? I am not convinced that this is a possible intention for God, who presumably knows perfectly well that any idea he causes will resemble both of his ideas equally strongly. He must know that the end result will be the same either way. So the conclusion seems to be that there can only *be* a difference between returning to the same place and visiting the other for the first time if the idea we get is identical with one of God's and not with the other. Otherwise the fact that our idea resembles both of God's will succeed in obliterating the difference entirely.

So there seem to be these two sorts of reasons for the stronger view that in perception we share the ideas of God. But maybe this view is impossible. Don't we know in advance that no two minds can have the same idea? Hylas makes this objection in the Third Dialogue:

But the same idea which is in my mind, cannot be in yours, or in any other mind. Doth it not therefore follow from your principles, that no two can see the same thing? And is not this highly absurd? (p. 247)

Hylas is in fact asking how it is possible for two ordinary people (created minds) to see the same thing. Surely, for idealism, objects consist of ideas, and an idea is restricted to a single mind. But the question is equally relevant to the possibility of our sharing ideas with God. In fact, we might think that it is if anything harder to answer. But Berkeley is entirely unsympathetic to the question:

But who sees not that all the dispute is about a word? to wit, whether what is perceived by different persons, may yet have the term *same* applied to it? (p. 248)

He continues by pointing out that the question whether a house that has been entirely rebuilt internally is the same one before and after is not a question about a matter of fact at all, since even when all the facts have been decided we will still have to seek an answer to it. And he concludes by suggesting that anybody who thinks otherwise is committed to an illegitimate abstract idea of identity. All this protestation makes me suspect that Berkeley felt uneasy on the point. And rightly so. Certainly if we have been right to stress the importance of the relations between space, continuity and reidentification, Berkeley cannot regard matters of reidentification as so trivial. But it may be that his thought can be reexpressed as follows. If we insist that a difference in owner marks a difference in idea, we must recognise that the imputed difference in idea is no more than the difference in owner. Now there may be a purpose in marking differences in owner in this way. We are in this way respecting the fact that minds are normally isolated from each other. Minds are isolated in the sense, among others, that no mind can directly affect the contents of any other. But once we realise that we are in this special case considering the relations between our mind and a unique mind which is not isolated from ours in that sort of way, we lose the normal reasons for counting ideas according to their owners. If I could directly cause you to see things my way just by willing it, we would lose the distinction between minds which we respect by considering the contents of a mind to be private to that mind. Our minds are not in that way distinct from God's, and there is therefore no justification for insisting that they cannot share their contents.

In this chapter we started with the suggestion that Berkeley has two arguments for the existence of God, one of which was rather dubious, and moved to the idea that he has only one, which combines in a perfectly acceptable way considerations of independence and of continuity. We then considered the more extreme suggestions that for Berkeley our knowledge of God's existence is not inferential knowledge; his existence is not the conclusion of an argument but more a matter of direct experience. There were two ways in which this might be made out. The first was to say that we distort our experience if we deny the existence of God, since only if there is a God can we make sense of our experience of the world as spatial. The second was to say that our experience of the world around us an experience of the ideas of God, so that we know that God exists because we have (some of) his ideas. In both these ways God comes closer to us in a way which Berkeley could only find agreeable.

5
Real Things

In the last chapter we considered various problems to do with Berkeley's God and his relation to the world, ending with the question whether our world is identical with or only a copy of a selection of the ideas in the mind of God. We now turn our attention more directly to Berkeley's account of the objects that make up the world.

According to Berkeley, those objects are collections of ideas. He writes:

And as several of these [ideas] are observed to accompany each other, they come to be marked by one name, and so to be reputed as one thing. Thus, for example, a certain colour, taste, smell, figure and consistence having been observed to go together, are accounted one distinct thing, signified by the name *apple*. Other collections of ideas constitute a stone, a tree, a book, and the like sensible things. (P. 1)

It is not perhaps clear whether Berkeley is talking here about the class of apples, for example (that is to say about the question why we group some objects and not others into sorts), or about some particular apple. But he shortly shows that he means to say that a particular object is a collection of ideas:

It is indeed an opinion strangely prevailing amongst men, that houses, mountains, rivers, and in a word all sensible objects have an existence natural or real, distinct from their being perceived by the understanding . . . Yet whoever shall find it in his heart to call it in question, may, if I mistake not, perceive it to involve a manifest contradiction. For what are the forementioned objects but . . . our own ideas or sensations? (P. 4)

We need to take this Berkeleian doctrine seriously, and ask whether it really makes sense. In particular, what alterations does it require in the way we think about the world and the objects that comprise it? We can approach this question by considering three difficulties raised for Berkeley by Jonathan Bennett.[1]

---

[1] See J. Bennett *Locke, Berkeley, Hume: Central Themes* (Oxford: Oxford University Press 1971), secs 33–4.

Interpersonal perception

We have already seen it suggested that Berkeley's world deprives us of one important feature, namely that it is possible for the same object to be perceived by more than one mind, whether at once or at different times. Berkeley has a choice between claiming that this is possible on his account, and claiming that though it is not possible this is not a very significant loss. His predilection for insisting that his theory detracts not at all from the reality of things leads him to prefer the former option. So what sense can he make of the notion that two people can see the same thing?

The natural first move is to try saying that this happens when two minds have very similar ideas. But this is hopeless; any similarity between ideas in different minds is neither necessary nor sufficient for those ideas to be ideas of the same thing.

Two ideas are ideas of the same thing if they are part of the same collection. So our question is which ideas in different minds are part of the same collection. But ideas of the same thing in different minds need not be similar; in fact they probably won't be. Suppose, just to take a simple example, that you and I are looking at the same object. That object will look one way to you and another to me, if only because we are looking at it from different angles. So similarity of ideas is not necessary for us to perceive the same object. But neither is it sufficient. I may be having egg-like ideas quite indistinguishable from those you are having, without this meaning that we are perceiving the same egg: this partly because, as Hume said, "nothing so like as eggs". So similarity of idea is really not much to do with identity of object. Locke knew this perfectly well. His account of two people seeing the same thing runs in terms of different ideas *caused* by one and the same object. This account can work because for Locke there are objects separable from the ideas they cause; ideas can therefore count as ideas *of* the same thing if they are ideas caused by the same thing. Now at one point in the Third Dialogue Berkeley may be claiming to be able to make the same move:

PHILONOUS: Your difficulty therefore, that no two see the same thing, makes equally against the materialists and me.
HYLAS: But they suppose an external archetype, to which referring their several ideas, they may truly be said to perceive the same thing.
PHILONOUS: And ... so may you suppose an external archetype on my principles; *external*, I mean, to your own mind; though indeed it must be supposed to exist in that mind which comprehends all things; but then this serves the ends of identity, as well as if it existed out of a mind. (p. 248)

What Berkeley is saying here depends on the notion of an archetype that he is using. If he means simply to copy the materialists' use, the thought is a causal thought. The idea would be that since God is the cause of our ideas, Berkeley can appeal to the identity of the cause of their ideas, just as Locke did, to secure the possibility of two people seeing the same thing. But, as it stands, this manifestly fails to work. Since God is the cause of all the ideas of sense, all objects of perception would end up identical; the problem now would be to avoid identity rather than to construct (or reconstruct) it. And we could not avoid this result by an appeal to the hope that some act or decision of God could determine which of the ideas he causes in us are to be ideas of the same thing. God is necessarily powerless in this respect; there is nothing he could do which would have this effect, since we have not yet constructed a distinction between those ideas which are of the same thing and those that are not, for God to manipulate in this way. Any divine stipulation that these two ideas are to be ideas of the same thing would be empty, since it would make no difference whatever.

It may be, however, that Berkeley means to take the notion of an archetype rather differently. Remember the point made at the end of the last chapter that our ideas of sense are not copies of but identical with ideas in the mind of God. If this is Berkeley's view, he can make a distinction between those ideas in different minds that are ideas of the same thing and those that are not. The first move is to point out that an idea in my mind can now be identical with one in yours, if they are both identical with one in the mind of God. This is not yet sufficient, for many ideas of the same thing will not be in this way identical; as we saw, the same object can and will look different to different minds. However, if the different ideas in the different minds are each identical with different ideas in God's mind, we can say that they are ideas of the same thing if the two ideas of God's are ideas of the same thing.

What then is it for two ideas of God's to be of the same thing? It looks as if the answer to this question must turn on some mirror in God's mind of the rare phenomenon of continuous perception of an object by us. But I think that this would be a mistake. For once we remember that what for us is perception is for God imagination, the appearance of mystery is dispelled. We ourselves have no trouble in imagining one object in different ways. It is a matter of free decision that the object of our imagination is one thing rather than several. And if we can do this, presumably God will be allowed to do it as well. So there is no genuine problem about how different ideas get to be ideas of one object in God's mind. And once this is allowed, we can say that the collection of different ideas in God's mind is the archetype for such ideas as we have of the same thing. This means that Berkeley can give an account of what it is for different ideas in two ordinary minds to be ideas of the same object, despite the apparent difficulties.)

Objects with a past and a future

Bennett argued that Berkeley could not give an account of interpersonal perception in a chapter that preceded, and hence made no mention of, any discussion of Berkeley's God and his role in the matter. That he concluded that Berkeley could give no account will therefore be hardly surprising. However there is a second difficulty which Bennett raises for Berkeley, from which it might seem harder to escape even with the help of God.

Our last problem was how to make sense of two people seeing the same object at the same time. But similar problems concern one person seeing the same object at different times. For that person's differently timed ideas to be ideas of the same thing, they must be part of the same collection. But what could make such ideas into part of one and the same collection?

Berkeley did not consider this problem, but presumably his reply would involve some appeal to ideas in the mind of God. The difficulty about such an appeal is that Berkeley conceives of God as incapable of change. Even if God exists somehow in time, he is not affected in any way by the temporal order. He does not have ideas one after another, but all together. So the temporal order of our ideas cannot mirror the order of those ideas in God's mind. What then can determine which ideas in the mind of God are ideas of the same object at different times, and which are ideas of different objects at the same time?

The answer to this question should emerge, I think, from previous thoughts about the power of God's imagination. For if we can imagine different temporal stages of one object as such, there seems to be no reason why God should not be able to do the same. Essentially, then, it is by the stipulation of God that ideas in his mind count as ideas of the same object at different times rather than as ideas of different objects at the same time.

So far the apparent difficulties have been resolved by recognising that our ideas of sense are identical with ideas in the mind of God. The next one is rather different.)

The distinction between reality and appearance

At the beginning of the last chapter we looked briefly at Berkeley's account of this distinction. Real things are those ideas which are "imprinted on the senses by the author of nature" (P. 33). I said, however, that we would return to it.

The first move here is to attempt to distinguish, and then to keep apart, two questions which are in danger always of being confused or of collapsing into each other. Both questions concern the distinction between reality and appearance. The first is like the question we asked about interpersonal perception. Our question there was not how we *know* when two of us are seeing the same object. Rather we were asking whether it was *possible* for two people to see the same object, on Berkeley's account. The danger was that Berkeley would be unable to draw any distinction between what we think of as two distinct cases, the first where two people see the same object and the second where they are seeing two indistinguishable objects, one for each of them. We concluded, however, that Berkeley could draw this distinction in his own way, and that therefore the realist had no advantage over him on this point. We could have gone on to ask the further question whether Berkeley's way of drawing the distinction gives a good account of how we know which of the two cases we are involved in at the moment. But having seen that Berkeley could at least draw the relevant distinction, we left this further question about knowledge unasked.

Similarly, our first question about the distinction between reality and appearance, or about the distinction between real things and mere appearances, is the question whether Berkeley is in a position to draw any such distinction at all. Won't everything whatever fall on the same side of this distinction, on the side of mere appearance? In this chapter we will consider only Berkeley's answer to this question, leaving the further question about how we know whether we are faced by a real thing this time or by a mere appearance for discussion in the next chapter. The latter is certainly a matter which we cannot shirk.

Berkeley sees the importance of showing how to distinguish reality from appearance, and his attempt to cope with the problem is worth quoting at length, even though we have seen it before. The problem as he sees it is expressed in *Principles* 34, as the first of a long list of objections which he rebuts one by one:

First then, it will be objected that by the foregoing principles, all that is real and substantial in Nature is banished out of the world: and instead thereof a chimerical scheme of ideas takes place. All things that exist, exist only in the mind, that is, they are purely notional. What therefore becomes of the sun, moon, and stars? . . . Are all these but so many chimeras and illusions on the fancy? . . . I answer, that by the principles premised, we are not deprived of any one thing in Nature. Whatever we see, feel, hear, or any wise conceive or understand, remains as secure as ever, and is as real as ever. There is a *rerum natura*, and the distinction between realities and chimeras retains its full force.

This is the realist charge that Berkeley's system would deprive the objects in the world of all reality. For if all such objects are merely ideas, surely the best we can say about the natural world is that it is a consistent appearance, and consistent appearance is just a different thing from there being real things around us. Of course when he speaks of real things, the realist uses his own conception of reality. He means that on Berkeley's system there are no objects that exist entirely independent of the mind. And this is true. But Berkeley's response is that he does not accept the realist's conception of what it is to be a real thing, for reasons to do with the argument from abstraction. Berkeley has his own conception of what it is to be a real thing, under which the very objects that the realist wanted to count as real do still emerge as real. This Berkeleian conception of the real emerged in the previous section:

The ideas imprinted on the senses by the Author of Nature are called *real things*: and those excited in the imagination being less regular, vivid and constant, are more properly termed *ideas*, or *images of things*, which they copy and represent . . . The ideas of sense are allowed to have more reality in them, that is, to be more strong, orderly, and coherent than the creatures of the mind; but this is no argument that they exist without the mind. They are also less dependent on the spirit, or thinking substance which perceives them, in that they are excited by the will of another and more powerful spirit. (P. 33)

Which of our ideas are real things? Berkeley's official answer is that the real things are the ideas of which we are not the cause (or at least not the main cause). The world we live in is real, because it is independent of us, the people who live in it and see it. But it is not independent of the mind in any stronger sense than that. For the real world still consists entirely of ideas. It is just that those ideas have a different cause; they occur in us, but are not caused by us. Since they need a cause, there can only be such ideas if there is another mind which has them and which is powerful enough to cause them in us, as we saw in chapter 4. But there is such a mind, and hence there can be real things in Berkeley's sense. So the realist is right to say that on Berkeley's system there are no real things, using a realist conception of reality, but wrong to say that Berkeley cannot find his own way of distinguishing between those ideas that are real things and those that are not.

Berkeley describes the distinction that we have been calling the distinction between reality and appearance as the distinction between the ideas of sense and those of the imagination. This is because there can only be two sorts of ideas, those of which we are the main cause and those of which we are not the main cause. Those of which we are not the main cause are the ideas of the imagination, and the rest are real things; there is no room for any third possibility. We might feel however that we do really need a richer conceptual apparatus than this. Crucially, we distinguish between ideas that are hallucinations or pure imagination, and ideas that are merely illusory. The drunkard who sees pink rats climbing up the wall sees something that is not real at all, but is the ✓ product of his own mind. Berkeley can cater for this well enough. But what about the much used example of the straight stick that looks bent in water? Is there a danger here that we have an idea which is not caused by us, but is not a real thing either? To say this would be to accept the need for a third category, which Berkeley could not produce. But Berkeley has seen this problem coming, and gives his answer in the Third Dialogue:

HYLAS: What say you to this? Since, according to you, men judge of the reality of things by their senses, how can a man be mistaken in thinking the moon a plain lucid surface, about a foot in diameter; or a square tower, seen at a distance, round; or an oar, with one end in the water, crooked?
PHILONOUS: He is not mistaken with regard to the ideas he actually perceives; but in the inferences he makes from his present perception. Thus in the case of the oar, what he immediately perceives by sight is certainly crooked; and so far he is in the right. But if he thence conclude, that upon taking the oar out of the water he shall perceive the same crookedness; or that it would affect his touch, as crooked things are wont to do: in that he is mistaken . . . His mistake lies not in what he perceives immediately and at present (it being a manifest contradiction to suppose he should err in respect of that) but in the wrong judgement he makes concerning the ideas he apprehends to be connected with those immediately perceived: or concerning the ideas that, from what he perceives at present, he imagines would be perceived in other circumstances. (p. 238)

According to this, the idea of the bent oar is as much part of the oar, part of a real thing, as are the more normal ideas of the oar as straight. Berkeley is consistent here. The idea which we call an illusion is not mainly caused by us, and is therefore a real thing; or rather it is part of a real thing, for objects such as oars are collections of ideas. Illusions, then, are parts of real things. We, as realists, would say that the oar is not really bent but merely appears to be bent. For Berkeley this sort of appearance is part of reality, not something to be set aside as unreal; the only way in which it differs from other ideas that we do not cause is that we need to be careful not to draw from it wrong inferences about the future and the past. In this sense Berkeley could agree that the oar merely *appears* to be bent and is not actually bent; but for him the mere appearance still counts as an idea of sense. So we should notice, without thinking of this as an objection to Berkeley, that his distinction between ideas of sense and ideas of the imagination is not quite our distinction between reality and appearance. But this still leaves his account of what it is for an idea to be (part of) a real thing intact.

There is however a further problem for Berkeley in this area, which concerns the claim that there are real things which we do not perceive. The account we have been considering asked merely which of *our* ideas are real things; it did not address the question whether there are any real things which are not ideas of ours. If there are, there must be a distinction between those ideas of God's which are real things and those which are not. God eternally perceives all possible ideas, traditionally. Which are the real things? The answer to this question cannot turn on our actual awareness, for two reasons. The first we have already seen; it is that there are now aspects of the world of which we created minds are not aware. The second concerns the Biblical story of the Creation, which maintains that God created the world before he created any finite minds to be aware of it. How could this be, if the real things are the ideas of sense in our minds? Berkeley is going to say that the created world is real because it is the one which God has decided to make it *possible* for created minds to perceive, though they are not yet actually perceiving it. But we shall not be in a position to assess this answer until we have considered a more extensive way in which the notion of the perceivable might replace that of the actually perceived in the account of what it is for an idea to be a real thing.

A further reason for considering use of the notion of the perceivable rather than that of the perceived or sensed has already surfaced implicitly in our examination of Bennett's objections to Berkeley. We noted earlier that Bennett raised those objections in such a way that the role of Berkeley's God was not allowed to be part of the answer to them; but that this was strange because the obvious Berkeleian answer was just one which relied on the existence of God as the persisting owner and cause of the ideas of sense. But this leaves us saying that those objections would have been effective against a form of idealism which made no appeal to a God. And I think that if this were true it would dramatically reduce the appeal of idealism in our secular age. The question then is whether a Berkeleian answer can be found to the three problems raised by Bennett which does not rely on the existence of God.

Before doing this it is worth pausing to make clear the exact sense in which Berkeley's idealism depends upon his God. We have been asking what room there is in Berkeley's system for our ordinary conceptions of the world as interpersonally perceivable, perceivable at different times, and containing real things rather than merely the creatures of the imagination. We found that Berkeley can hold that one idea can be present to two perceiving minds, that two ideas at different times can be ideas of the same object, and that real things can be understood as those ideas which are more independent of the mind that perceives them. Berkeley's position, then, has room for a world that is public, persisting and real. The important point is that no mention of God was made in the account of what it is for an object to be public, persisting or real. In the case of reality, for example, we did not say that an idea is a real thing if it is caused by God, but that it counts as a real thing if it is less dependent on the mind that perceives it. Similarly, two people can perceive the same thing, not if they are related in a certain way to the mind of God, but simply if they have an idea or ideas which is or are part of one thing. So far, then, God plays no role; his existence and contribution is not mentioned in our account of what it is for there to be real things. But when we reach the question whether there are any things of that sort, Berkeley's answer depends crucially upon God's contribution. For instance, it turns out that the only way there can be ideas which are less dependent on the mind that perceives them is if there is a mind which is God who is the main cause of them.

One way to express this point is to say that though the existence and contribution of God is no part of what we mean when we talk about real things, there can in fact be no real things unless there is God. Our metaphysics depends upon God, but our semantics (theory of meaning) does not. And this means that though God is vitally important to Berkeley, we must be careful not to overemphasise or misplace his importance when we ask how well idealism might fare without God.

Idealism and phenomenalism

To approach this question we need to distinguish between the idealism which is Berkeley's official doctrine and a close relative, phenomenalism. The idealist holds that objects are collections of actual ideas, ideas actually existing in some mind. The phenomenalist holds that objects are collections of actual and possible ideas, ideas that either are existing or at least could exist in some mind. Although these positions look similar, there is a crucial difference between them. For the idealist, an object only exists so long as some mind is actually perceiving it, while for the phenomenalist an object exists so long as it is possible for it to be perceived, even if no mind is perceiving it at the moment. Thus, in a world without God, objects would have to be thought of by the idealist as having at best a gappy existence. But the phenomenalist can ascribe to them a continuous existence, since it is all the time possible that they be perceived. This reveals one reason why phenomenalism is thought of as an improvement on idealism. Its recognition that the possibility of perception is sufficient for the existence of a material object renders it a more flexible and more attractive position, which still retains the core of the idealist insistence that material objects cannot be conceived as able to have an existence out of all relation with the mind. This at least is the standard opinion; but we shall find reasons to doubt some parts of it.

The first thing we must show is that phenomenalism can cope Godlessly with Bennett's three objections. We have already seen how it can ascribe continuity to the material world without for that reason needing to discover a persisting perceiver. So long as it remains possible for the world to be perceived, it retains all the existence it could ever hope to have, on phenomenalist principles.

On interpersonal perception, presumably the phenomenalist approach is to say that though actual ideas may be counted according to the minds that have them, leaving it hard for the idealist to say how two minds can perceive the same real thing, a possible idea is not to be individuated in this way by the minds for which it is possible. It is the same idea that is available to both of us, not in the sense that we may both have it, but in the sense that it may be either one of us that has it, depending on who gets into the right place and looks. For two people to see the same object, then, is for them both to have ideas which are part of the same collection of possibilities. But haven't we simply relocated our question? Don't we now have to ask what it is for two ideas to be part of the same collection of possibilities? We do, but there is a phenomenalist answer. A group of possible ideas is collected up so as to count as one material thing if there is a single well-unified explanation of their occurrence, an explanation running in terms of the way these ideas figure in a fabric of possibilities. What unifies such a fabric? Our experience tells us that ideas occur in regular patterns. For instance, I know that fires regularly burn those who put their hands in them. I see you putting your hand in the fire, and you are burnt; I know that if I had done that, I would have been burnt. This is what it is for ideas in different minds to be ideas of the same thing. They occur as part of a single pattern, interrelated in the regular way that experience has made us familiar with.

On the question what it is to have ideas at different times of one and the same object, the phenomenalist is in a stronger position. The availability of possible ideas between the times of the actual ideas keeps the object in existence, as we have said, and shows which differently timed ideas count as ideas of the same object. My idea of a tree now and my idea of it in five minutes' time are ideas of the same tree if there are ideas of a certain sort which I might have had if I had stayed where I was and kept looking in the same direction. The fact that I would have continued to have the right sort of ideas if I had bothered is what makes my differently timed ideas into ideas of the same tree. And the same sort of reply works for an object that does not stay so much the same as a tree does, for instance a fire in a fireplace. The marked difference between one's first idea of a fire and one's last (the hot ash) does not prevent them being ideas of the same fire, because this sort of progression is just what our experience leads us to expect. The changing fire is an unified pattern of possibilities, a pattern of a sort with which we are perfectly familiar and which explains the occurrence of any idea within the relevant collection.

On the distinction between appearance and reality, the phenomenalist can agree with and extend Berkeley's use of the criteria of strength, orderliness and coherence. We have already seen the phenomenalist use these criteria in his account of a single enduring object of interpersonal perception. The fact that a single idea fits well into a pattern of other ideas we have had and that that pattern is well represented in our experience is good evidence that the idea is part of a real thing. We have to admit, however, that no matter how well an actual idea fits the pattern of other actual ideas, it may still not be (part of) a real thing. Our criteria are not foolproof here. The idealist maintains that reality is not constituted by those criteria; what it is for an object to be real is for it to be an idea or collection of ideas that are causally independent of the mind that perceives them. The phenomenalist agrees that reality is not constituted by the criteria of strength, orderliness and coherence; no matter how strong, orderly and coherent our actual ideas, there still remains the possibility that they are not a real thing – that things are not the way they seem to us to be. But this could only be because there are other ideas that we could have had and which would not have fitted, and would have destroyed the orderliness and coherence of what we have so far. Reality is constituted by regular and coherent patterns of possibilities. There is no chance that an idea should fail to be (part of) a real thing if it is part of a regular pattern of possible ideas.

An example will help here. Suppose that I am lost in the desert, dying of thirst. My tortured brain conceives an hallucination of a shady oasis, complete with pool and palm trees; this mirage is entirely the result of my fevered imagination. I redouble my efforts, and succumb to them; I die in the attempt to reach a place which is merely a figment of my own imagination, not God's. This sorry tale reveals the difference between idealism and phenomenalism, and how idealism finds it necessary to use God to make reality possible. For if we suppose in addition that nobody else ever ventures into that part of the desert, we are supposing that no actual idea ever occurs out of order with or incoherent with my idea of the oasis. This means that my illusion, being completely coherent with all other actual ideas, would have to count as a real thing were it not for Berkeley's extra, causal question whether those ideas were comparatively independent of me, the mind that perceived them. But Berkeley can only answer this question by appeal to God; and so for an idealism without God, coherent illusion would be the same as reality. For the phenomenalist, on the other hand, my illusion is not in danger of counting as a real thing merely because of its coherence with all other actual ideas. It would only count as real if it were coherent with all the other ideas that people might have had. Of course other people might go or have gone to that place, and they would then have had ideas inconsistent with mine; this is what renders my ideas an illusion, and it does so without the help of any God. And if when those other people had got there they would have had ideas like mine, and if, had they seemed to reach the oasis, they would have had ideas of palm trees and cool pools (etc. etc.), then, the phenomenalist would insist, their ideas and mine would have been real things. There is nothing more to reality, according to phenomenalism, than the possibility of regular, coherent experience.

These, then, are the phenomenalist's answers to Bennett's questions. It may be that they are not perfect, but it does seem that they do show the possibility of a position which is not far away from Berkeley's official view, and which has the added attraction of being able to get by without the dubious reliance on a God for whose existence the arguments cannot be called watertight. Why, then, was Berkeley an idealist rather than a phenomenalist?

The trouble is that it is not so clear that he did reject phenomenalism in favour of idealism. Berkeley did not know our names for the two positions, but as soon as we are alert for expressions of preference we find that he sometimes speaks as if he were a phenomenalist, and sometimes as if he were an idealist. He starts the *Principles* with what should be his official position:

It is evident to any one who takes a survey of the objects of human knowledge, that they are either ideas actually imprinted on the senses, or . . . (P. 1)

Note the word 'actually' here. In similar vein, he writes:

that all the choir of heaven and furniture of the earth, in a word all those bodies which compose the mighty frame of the world, have not any subsistence without a mind, that their being is to be perceived or known; that consequently so long as they are not actually perceived by me, or do not exist in my mind or that of any other created spirit, they must either have no existence at all, or else subsist in the mind of some eternal spirit. (P. 6)

The first half of this sentence could be an expression either of phenomenalism or of idealism, but the second half is explicitly idealist; only from within an idealist perspective would the argument by remainder which it contains go through. And of course we should remember in all this Berkeley's slogan *'Esse est Percipi'* (to be is to be perceived). This slogan is repeated in various places, and alluded to in the passage quoted above; it is quite distinct from any phenomenalist slogan, which would be *'Esse est Percipi Posse'* (to be is to be perceivable). However there are other passages where Berkeley seems to speak as a phenomenalist, the first of which occurs between the two quoted already:

The table I write on, I say, exists, that is, I see and feel it; and if I were out of my study I should say it existed, meaning thereby that if I was in my study I might perceive it, or that some other spirit actually does perceive it. (P. 3)

The conditional clause "if I was in my study I might perceive it" expresses a phenomenalist thought; for Berkeley to think of some other spirit's actually perceiving it as an acceptable alternative to the possibility of his doing so, he is thinking in phenomenalist terms. Another splendidly phenomenalist passage is:

the question, whether the earth moves or no, amounts in reality to no more than this, to wit, whether we have reason to conclude from what hath been observed by astronomers, that if we were placed in such and such circumstances, and such or such a position and distance, both from the earth and sun, we should perceive the former to move among the choir of the planets, and appearing in all respects like one of them. (P. 58)

This is a phenomenalist remark because it says that the earth's movement consists just in the availability or possibility of certain ideas; this is a phenomenalist rather than an idealist account of reality. The last evidence of phenomenalist tendencies comes in the discussion of the Biblical account of the Creation in the Third Dialogue:

All objects are eternally known by God, or which is the same thing, have an eternal existence in his mind: but when things before imperceptible to creatures, are by a decree of God, made perceptible to them; then are they said to begin a relative existence, with respect to created minds. (p. 252)

Here Berkeley suggests that for a real thing to exist is for it to be perceptible to us, not perceived by us. Talk of the perceptible rather than of the perceived is just what we would expect from a phenomenalist.

So the evidence is conflicting, and I think that we have to admit that

Berkeley was not as clear in his own mind on this topic as we could wish. This leaves it up to our own devices. If the text is not decisive, what reasons can we provide from within Berkeley's thought that should have led him one way or the other? Here we are not asking which is the better position, but which is the more consistent with Berkeley's argumentation elsewhere.

One suggestion is that one Berkeleian argument for God only goes through if Berkeley is an idealist. This is the continuity argument. We could not argue from:

Real things continue to exist when unperceived by any created spirit

to

There must be an infinite spirit to perceive them during the gaps in our awareness of them

if we supposed that mere perceivability was sufficient for the existence of material things. But this approach is a bit broken-backed, because, as we have seen, it is dubious whether Berkeley does employ a continuity argument in this crude form. If continuity plays a role in argument for God's existence, it is a rather more subtle role than this. On the other side there is the point that Berkeley's account of the Creation seems to need a phenomenalist version of what happened when God created the material world. Perhaps, then, this approach is not going to help us much either. A more promising line is the thought that the reason why Berkeley is cavalier about the distinction between idealism and phenomenalism is not that he hasn't clearly seen its importance, but that he doesn't accept the distinction. The contrast between actual and merely possible ideas is not one that he can think makes sense. If this were true, and in particular if its truth depends crucially on the role of God in Berkeley's system, we can see why he shifts indifferently from one form of expression to another, and also perhaps accept that phenomenalism is preferable while seeing why Berkeley remained an idealist.

There are three distinct reasons for thinking that Berkeley wanted to collapse the distinction between actual and possible ideas. The first is that he actually says so in the Third Dialogue:

And what is perceivable but an idea? And can an idea exist without being actually perceived? (p. 234)

Here Berkeley seems to be saying that all possible ideas are actual ideas. No idea can be merely possible. So material objects cannot be collections of actual and possible ideas; or rather they can, but this is no different from their being collections of actual ideas. Phenomenalism and idealism collapse into each other. But what is Berkeley's reason for saying this? There may be some thought like this going on, that every possible idea is an idea, and every idea is an actual idea. But this is not true in a general way; we cannot say in general that any possible F is an F and therefore an actual F. For instance, if I get married I may have a son; there is a possible son for me. But we would not wish to conclude from this that if I get married there is (already) an actual son who may be mine. So Berkeley's reason here cannot lie in some general relation between the actual and the possible.

Let us abandon this thought for a moment and consider a different approach. It may be that it is the existence of Berkeley's God that collapses the distinction between actual and possible ideas. For if God eternally perceives all possible ideas, every possible idea is an actual idea in some mind, namely the mind of God. There is no reason for Berkeley to trouble himself, therefore, about the distinction between actual and possible. There is no practical difference between saying that for a material object to exist is for it to be perceived and saying that it is for it to be perceivable. For everything that is perceivable is perceived, or at least exists in some mind. (Remember that God does not strictly speaking perceive the ideas of sense; he imagines them. God is senseless, i.e. devoid of senses if not of sense.)

Why does Berkeley believe that God eternally perceives every possible idea? Is it because God is omnipotent? Presumably not, because to be omnipotent is to be able to do anything, not actually to be doing everything; the latter does not make sense anyway. It must therefore be God's omniscience which is at issue. There are two ways in which this might emerge. First, we might say that in virtue of his omniscience God knows everything possible as well as everything actual. But then the question why this is so would simply recur. The second route is to say that for God there is just no distinction between the possible and the actual. This seems to be nearer the mark, but it is no answer to our question. For we were asking why this was so, and it is no answer to be told that it is.

What is more, the appeal to God's eternal awareness of everything possible may turn out to be irrelevant to our question. For the decision whether the existence of material objects consists in their being perceived or merely perceivable is not affected by the independent discovery that everything that is perceivable is also perceived. Our problem is how to conceive of material existence; the existence of God as eternal perceiver of all possibilities does not collapse the distinction between the perceivable and the perceived, but merely tells us that, whatever decision we make, the existence of the material world will be as enduring as God allows it to be.

It seems to me that we have not yet discovered a reasonable reason for Berkeley to think that the choice between phenomenalism and idealism is empty. There remains however the possibility that the reason for saying that all possible ideas are actual is not a general reason, derived from some general relation between the possible and the actual, but a special reason derived from what it is to conceive of an idea as merely possible. We should remember in this connection the conclusion of Berkeley's argument from the impossibility of abstraction, namely that we cannot conceive of an object either as existing unconceived or as able to exist unconceived. If this is his position it is rigidly anti-phenomenalist. For the phenomenalist is maintaining that we can make sense of the mere possibility of perception; that possibility exists, or those possibilities exist, whether they are perceived or not. To conceive of something as existing if it is merely able to be perceived is implicitly to conceive of something as able to exist unconceived.

Another way of putting what I think is the same point, and which emerged in our discussion of abstraction at the end of chapter 3, is to say that we cannot abstract from an idea its mental aspect, and suppose that the remainder is capable of independent existence. And we cannot suppose either that this remainder does exist unconceived, or that it *could* exist unconceived. It is like trying to conceive of a pain which is not hurting anybody. We cannot suppose that the pain either does exist or is capable of existing except in some mind. And similarly we cannot suppose that there are ideas which nobody has got but which someone could have, because this is to think of these ideas as existing in mere possibility. The only things of which we can conceive are therefore ideas, and we can only conceive of those ideas as actually present in some mind. Nothing less (or more) than this is possible.

This means that Berkeley's real reason for thinking that the distinction between idealism and phenomenalism collapses is the same as his reason for thinking realism incoherent or contradictory. It imputes a pleasing unanimity to his position at its very centre. Phenomenalism emerges as either indistinguishable from idealism, or, if distinguishable, as defective for exactly the same trenchant reasons as Berkeley brought to play against Locke's realism; the phenomenalist, if occuping a distinct position, is convicted of attempting just the same impossible feats of abstraction as the realist. And this has the result that we cannot suppose that phenomenalism is an improvement on idealism, for the basic motive for adopting idealism is one that is inconsistent with phenomenalism, indeed one which renders phenomenalism incoherent. We have pretended along the way that the two positions are close, and that the motivation for one is not much different from that for the other. But it now seems that this is a mistake, and that given Berkeley's reasons for his idealist stance it would be impossible for him to broaden his position and adopt, perhaps thankfully as Bennett would suppose, the advantages of flexibility which we have seen attending phenomenalism's use of the distinction between actual and possible ideas. If either of the two positions is internally consistent, it is the more extreme rather than the more conciliatory: as so often happens in philosophy. The only way to render phenomenalism acceptable or attractive is to find for it an entirely different motivation than that for idealism. We shall consider in the next chapter the question whether there are not some epistemological advantages shared by both theories: advantages, that is to say, in the attempt to make sense of our ability to come to know about the world around us. But even if this were true, it could not by itself justify the adoption of either. As Berkeley is so fond of emphasising, it is not the ease with which idealism shows the possibility of empirical knowledge that is crucial. It is the impossibility of conceiving of the world in the realist's way or in the phenomenalist's way. Epistemological advantages are additional extras rather than the main menu.

Why, if phenomenalism is inconsistent with his idealist motivation, does Berkeley allow himself to talk so often in phenomenalist terms? It must be remembered that we have concluded that phenomenalism is only unacceptable if distinct from idealism. If we take it that all possible ideas are actual ideas, there is nothing wrong with phenomenalist expressions from an idealist point of view. Our position is that Berkeley doesn't care about the distinction between the two views because for him they are indistinguishable, not that because there is such an enormous difference between them that he ought to be more careful to avoid any taint of phenomenalism.

Haven't we admitted, however, that Berkeley's only method of accounting for the Biblical version of the Creation is to speak in phenomenalist terms of how "things before imperceptible to creatures are by a decree of God made perceptible to them"? There is a special difficulty about the Creation, as we saw. It derives from the fact that God is held in the Biblical account to have created the world before he created any finite spirits to perceive it. The question is what difference the Creation can have made, on Berkeley's account. What change occurred at the moment of Creation? God's eternal awareness of every possible idea is part of this problem, not part of the answer to it. The problem concerns what happens when he chooses some of those ideas to be the real things, and it is exacerbated by the doctrine that God himself is not subject to change. In my view it is the latter doctrine that is the cause of the fix Berkeley finds himself in. For without it Berkeley can say without embarrassment that God at the Creation chooses one infinite pattern of ideas as the one which he will reveal to created minds. Later we will see that this decision could alternatively be described as the decision to adopt a certain language. Berkeley argues that we can think of the world as God's language, the way in which he speaks to us and tells us what is going to happen and what has happened. Using this, why shouldn't we say that at the Creation God decides which language he will talk to the minds he is to create tomorrow or the day after?

If this is the answer to the question about the Creation, what should we say about the other problem raised at the end of the last section, whether there are real things of which no created mind is aware? We have already concluded that for Berkeley the distinction between idealism and phenomenalism is empty. But this does not answer our question here, for it does not tell us whether to hold that the only real things are those perceived by finite spirits. The real point is the point about independence. An idea of ours is a real thing if it is suitably independent of us, and any other idea which is available to us and has that sort of independence is (part of) a real thing. The real world consists of such ideas, and it exists continuously because they exist continuously in the mind of God. But it is not his awareness of them, nor our actual awareness that is required for reality, but the independence that the ideas would have if we were aware of them. Reality and independence are inextricably linked, but they are linked thus much more for us than they are for God. For us the ideas of sense are more real, on Berkeley's showing, than are the ideas of our own imagination. There is an immense difference between the two. But for God this is not so. For him the distinction between the world of real things and the other worlds which are *only* figments of his imagination is nothing like so important, being merely a matter of which ones he decides to make available to finite minds.

Idealism, anti-realism, and God

We asked earlier whether Berkeley's idealism could survive without its God, and our conclusion now seems to be that it can't. God was an important part of the idealist reply to Bennett's three objections, and although phenomenalism could handle those objections without God, it was misguided to say that idealism could without any real loss be expanded into phenomenalism, because the latter is inconsistent with Berkeley's main argument for idealism. So the position now seems to be that Bennett's objections show the extent to which idealism, in Berkeley's hands, needs God if it is to be plausible at all.

Idealism and phenomenalism are two forms of anti-realism. But there are other forms too. What all the forms have in common is that they reject the realist's attitude that the world is one on which we have at best a tentative grasp. For them, the world is somehow constituted by the sorts of ways in which it does or at least could appear to us. More modern forms of anti-realism maintain that truth consists in that for which we have or could have sufficient evidence, or that to understand a proposition is to know what things would look like if it were true, that is, to know how to verify it. All such positions have a tendency to reduce the size of the world, for there are some propositions which the realist would say may or may not be true, but which lie quite beyond *our* range. This is because the world, for the realist, has its existence quite independent of our grasp on it. This being so, there can be parts or aspects of the world on which we are unable to get any grasp at all. Anti-realism, viewed now in general, denies this, and is therefore in danger of contracting the world by restricting it to those elements on which we can get some grasp. All other elements are to be abandoned as inconceivable. Anti-realists differ in their attitude to this. Some view it with equanimity, others with some alarm. Berkeley was in the latter camp. His tendency was always to claim that his form of anti-realism detracted nothing from the reality of things, and in general that we lose nothing of our familiar world by recognising the truth of his principles. Others maintain frankly that the realist's world is overblown, and should be cut down to size – our size. But because of the reducing tendency of anti-realism, anti-realists who want to say that nothing is really lost by coming to understand the world on their principles have to find some way of re-expanding the world to get it back to size. Berkeley achieves this by the judicious use of God as the sort of infinite perceiver who can, by his awareness, keep in existence any aspect of the world on which *our* grasp is defective. For instance, the reality of the remote past and of the future are securely established by God's 'present' awareness of them. And this sort of manoeuvre is endemic in anti-realism. We re-expand the world by conceiving of a vastly more powerful perceiver than ourselves, but one still somehow like ourselves. A perceiver who can perceive all times at once, or who is immediately aware of the contents of every other mind, gives us a conception of those times and those contents as objects on which there could be a grasp like ours, and thus stifles any anti-realist qualms about those objects as real parts of the world. So the tendency which Berkeley clearly evinces, of re-expanding the world to realist proportions by use of an infinite perceiver, is a classic move in anti-realism, one to which phenomenalism and other modern forms of anti-realism are equally prone. You pay your money here and you take your choice. First you have to decide whether to accept idealist or anti-realist strictures on the possibility of a reality on which we have no grasp. Then you have to decide whether you are willing to accept the sort of reduction of the size of the world that this seems to bring with it. Berkeley was not, and used God for what he saw as necessary reinflation.

The conclusion, then, is that if idealism is to retain every aspect of a conceptual scheme designed for realists by realists, it is going to need to introduce something like Berkeley's God. Some realists will feel that this leaves idealism with an awkward choice between two implausibilities: God, or a large reduction in the world. Berkeley would not think of this as a criticism.

In this chapter we have considered whether Berkeley's account of the reality of the world can be defended against various objections, and if so whether any appeal to God is necessary in this defence or whether a secular variant of Berkeley's theory can be constructed to suit a secular age. The secular variant which we considered was phenomenalism, but we concluded that, if this is a genuinely distinct position, it is in the end incompatible with Berkeley's central argument for his idealism, and so that Berkeley needs God if his idealism is to work.

What we are left with is an idealist account of real things as independent of us, but not in the sense that a realist would give to this phrase. Real things are just those ideas which we share with another mind which causes them in us. Their independence is an independence from *our* awareness of them, not an absolute independence from all minds whatever. We can make no sense of the realists' idea that objects might have an existence entirely independent of all minds. Instead we must say that there can only be real things if there is a mind with the right sort of powers, a Godlike mind which selects from among the ideas of which it is continuously aware some which we are to share with it. So for Berkeley, reality and God stand and fall together.

6

Perception and Knowledge

In chapter 2 we distinguished two forms of scepticism. The first and weaker urged that knowledge is impossible for us. The second and stronger urged that we do not even understand the propositions whose truth we are, according to the first, unable to know. I suggested earlier that Berkeley was very much more interested in arguments of the second sort, in the sense that he used such arguments against his chosen target, the realist. We shall in due course (in chapter 9) come to see this sort of argument turned against Berkeley himself. But Berkeley does also use, though less tenaciously, arguments of the first sort, and clearly thought that realism is vulnerable to them. They do, after all, express his feeling that realism leaves the world too distant from us, beyond our grasp. He must therefore have taken it that his own position does contain an answer to them. It would hardly be reasonable to throw insults at the realist for failing to show how it is possible for us to have any perceptual knowledge if one's own theory fares no better on this score. Berkeley was in fact so convinced of the superiority of his idealism here that the full title he gave to the *Principles* was: "A Treatise concerning the Principles of Human Knowledge, wherein the chief causes of error and difficulty in the *Sciences*, with the grounds of *Scepticism*, *Atheism*, and *Irreligion*, are inquired into". The *Dialogues* have a similar title: "Three Dialogues between Hylas and Philonous, in Opposition to Sceptics and Atheists". There is a lot of trumpeting going on here, and in this chapter we shall be asking whether it is justified.

In considering the claims of scepticism, Berkeley was not interested so much in the completely general claim that we can have no knowledge at all, but rather in the claim that we can have no knowledge about the world around us. This sort of scepticism focuses on perception and perceptual knowledge. Berkeley held that his system retains the possibility of perceptual knowledge, while realism makes such knowledge impossible.

To see this, we can return to the first argument against representative realism that we considered in chapter 2. It ran as follows:

But though it were possible that solid, figured, moveable substances may exist without the mind, corresponding to the ideas we have of bodies, yet how is it possible for us to know this? Either we must know it by sense, or by reason. As for our senses, by them we have the knowledge only of our sensations, ideas, or those things that are immediately perceived by sense, call them what you will: but they do not inform us that things exist without the mind, or unperceived, like to those which are perceived . . . It remains therefore that if we have any knowledge at all of external things, it must be by reason, inferring their existence from what is immediately perceived by sense. But what reason can induce us to believe the existence of bodies without the mind, from what we perceive, since the very patrons of matter themselves do not pretend, there is any necessary connexion betwixt them and our ideas? I say it is granted on all hands . . . that it is possible we might be affected with all the ideas we have now, though no bodies existed without, resembling them. (P. 18)

And he concludes:

In short, if there were external bodies, it is impossible we should ever come to know it; and if there were not, we might have the very same reasons to think there were that we have now. (P. 20)

We have already noticed, in chapter 2, that this argument is as it stands not an attack on Locke's representative realism, but on a different account of perception, which we called inferential realism. This is because Berkeley assumes that his realist opponent will admit that we are never aware of physical objects, and that the only things of which we are aware are those of which we are immediately aware, namely our own ideas. But the representative realist claims rather that we are immediately aware of our own ideas, and thereby mediately of physical objects. Our awareness of those objects is still perceptual awareness, for the representative realist, and not inferential knowledge. So the representative realist keeps the world closer to us than does his inferentialist rival; he generates a sense in which we do genuinely *see* the world, rather than simply work out that it must be there.

It seems then that Berkeley has mistaken his target. He might still want to argue that representative realism condemns us to perceptual ignorance, but he will have to find another way of doing it. What is more, it must be very different from the argument quoted above. For that argument contains a move which looks distinctly fallacious. Berkeley suggests that since it is possible that we should have our ideas "though no bodies existed without, resembling them", the occurrence of ideas in us cannot help us to know that there are such things as bodies. But we might be tempted to reply that the mere fact that it is possible that we should have the ideas we have in the absence of a physical world does little to show that we have no knowledge of that world. What is at issue for

Locke, and for the inferential realist too, is whether it is *probable* that there be such a world around us causing our ideas, and it can of course be probable that this is so while remaining possible that it is not.

Berkeley has an answer to this charge, which he gives in *Principles* 19. But the point that I want to make now is that our discussion of perceptual knowledge and scepticism has so far failed really to engage with Berkeley's concerns. The complaints we have made about his arguments, though reasonable enough in their own way, have appeared more effective than they really are because they have ignored a basic assumption common to both Locke and Berkeley.

God's knowledge and our knowledge

We saw in chapter 2 one basic assumption common to both philosophers, namely empiricism; and we came eventually to describe Berkeley's attack on Locke's metaphysics as the charge that empiricism and realism are incompatible. The position is similar when we turn from metaphysics to epistemology. I take my start from the full version of the title to the *Three Dialogues*, which appeared only in the first two editions. It was:

Three Dialogues Between Hylas and Philonous, the design of which is plainly to demonstrate the reality and perfection of human knowledge, the incorporeal nature of the soul, and the immediate providence of a Deity: in opposition to Sceptics and Atheists. Also to open a method for rendering the Sciences more easy, useful and compendious.

The question I want to start with is what it means for human knowledge to be real and perfect. The answer to this question reveals an assumption common to both Locke and Berkeley, and generally in the intellectual tradition in which they were working. Man is made in the image of God. This statement was taken as true, but as a truth concerning man's mind rather than his body. This means that the intellectual powers ascribed to man are to be modelled on those ascribed to God, and seen always in relation to those of God. Human knowledge, in particular, if available at all, is seen as the same sort of thing as God has. Of course God has infinitely more of this knowledge; he knows much more than we do. But genuine knowledge, when we get it, is exactly the thing that God has. If God knows something and we know it too, we are in just the same state as he is, as far as this item is concerned.

A state can only count as knowledge, therefore, if it is the state God would be in. If it falls short of that Godlike state in any way, it is not true knowledge. Now in some areas there was general agreement that we can attain this Godlike state without too much difficulty. For instance, some simple truths in mathematics are known by us, and our relation to those truths is just the same as God's. Locke called our knowledge of these truths intuitive; by this he seems to have meant that we can just see them to be true straight off, in the very way that God does. But in other areas there is more dispute. Two such areas which will concern us are, first, scientific knowledge, which we will discuss in the next chapter, and second perceptual knowledge. Can we have perceptual knowledge? Not unless the state we would be in if we had it would be identical with God's relation to the truths about the world around us that we are hoping to know by observation, i.e. by use of our senses. But how could it be? God has no senses; he knows these truths directly, while our knowledge is necessarily mediated by our senses. The use of the senses can thus come to seem a sort of disadvantage, ruling us out from having real and perfect knowledge of the things around us. The state we are in when we see that it is raining is a mediated state, which can never be identical with God's direct awareness of facts which are transparently present to him.[1]

So both Berkeley and Locke were working in a tradition which itself rendered perceptual knowledge problematic. One attempt to resolve the problem was made by Newton, who suggested that space and time are God's sensorium. The sensorium was supposed to be the mental space in which we perceive our ideas. So God does more or less have senses, on this hopeful account, though they are very different from ours; and this removes the main general difficulty, though at the cost of inserting some others. Berkeley, as we will see, has a much better answer.

What account is to be given of God's knowledge? Various answers are possible within the tradition, but Berkeley's tendency is to think of God's knowledge, in every area, as an idealisation of perceptual knowledge. Things which we can only hope to know by inference, God can somehow see straight off: this whether we are thinking of general scientific laws, facts about the past and future, or complex truths in mathematics. After all, if man is made in God's image, the best state possible for us must be something like God's; otherwise it would be a pretty poor image. In mathematics, perhaps our best state is where we simply see some truth straight off. So God's knowledge must be always like that.

One might be pardoned the thought that there is a deep incoherence in this general view, which takes our perceptual knowledge as inherently unsatisfactory and less perfect than God's, and then claims that God's

---

[1] See E. J. Craig 'Philosophy and philosophies', *Philosophy* 1983, 58, pp. 189–201. I am grateful to Bob Hargrave for this reference, and for making me see the importance of this background assumption.

knowledge is everywhere perceptual. But the view itself was not so much the subject for explicit debate as a background assumption, and defects in background assumptions tend not to be exposed by ordinary argument, but rather to emerge slowly as the background itself begins to change.[2]

With all this in hand we can return to Berkeley's argument against Locke. The first thing to say is that Locke's representative realism is a great improvement on inferential realism, so far as concerns the attempt to say that in perception we can achieve a state not dissimilar to God's. To say that our knowledge of our surroundings is a matter of inference was manifestly to distinguish it from any knowledge that God might have of the same things. At least Locke's approach avoids this danger. But Berkeley's complaint is that it still does not go far enough. His point can be the one we have already made, that a mediated awareness can never be identical with, and must always be less perfect than, an unmediated or direct awareness. On Locke's own showing, therefore, our perceptual awareness of our surroundings is always lacking something, and cannot be real and perfect knowledge.

We can also now see why Berkeley's charge that it is always possible that the world should not be the way it seems to us to be turns out to be more relevant than we first thought. For a state of which this is true is less perfect than one of which it is not true. God's direct awareness of an object such as a tree is a state in which the tree is transparently present to him, a state which could not occur unless the tree were indeed there. Our state, by contrast, is one which could occur in the absence of the tree. Our state is therefore less perfect than God's, and cannot be real and perfect knowledge. This argument, so far as it goes, is as effective against representative realism as it is against inferential realism. Both theories suppose that our perceptual awareness is in the relevant sense imperfect, and are therefore committed to admitting that it is not perfect knowledge.

So Berkeley's arguments against Locke make more sense than we at first admitted. It now remains for us to see how his own approach does better. As I said, though Berkeley does not put so much stress on perceptual scepticism as he does upon strong sceptical arguments, he still wants to claim that in this area he does dramatically better than does his realist opponent, to the extent of blazoning it all over the title page. So what advantages does his idealism offer?

We said that perfect knowledge is available only where there is no possibility that things should be other than they seem. But how could one

---

[2] This is one of the general theses of T. Kuhn *The Structure of Scientific Revolutions* (Chicago: Chicago University Press 1970).

hope to eliminate this possibility? It can only be removed entirely if the way things seem is identical with the way they are: that is, if what is present to the mind (what seems) just is the nature of the object (what is). This is how things are for God, and on Berkeley's account it is how things can be for us too. When we have an idea which is part of a real thing, our idea (how things seem to us) is part of the object (what is). We can therefore have an awareness of the object which is no less direct than God's, and so our knowledge that the object exists and of what it is like is, at least in this respect, as good as God's. We can have real and perfect knowledge.

It is worth remembering in this connection the view we attributed to Berkeley in chapter 4, that our ideas of sense are identical with ideas in the mind of God. This meant that the objects of our perceptual states can be identical with those of God's. Now we also see that our states with respect to those objects can be identical with God's too. The only relevant difference between God and us is that he is in those states because he chooses to be (we expressed this before by saying that God doesn't perceive but only imagines), while we are in them mainly because he chooses that we should be. But this is an external difference, which does not detract from the identity of the states themselves.

This means that Berkeley's account of perception is one on which the senses are not a hindrance or mediating barrier between us and the world we are trying to see. Given the underlying assumption of what it is for knowledge to be perfect, Berkeley's position is genuinely superior to Locke's in the way he claims.

Does this mean that Berkeley has found an answer to the sort of sceptical arguments current nowadays, which are different in style to those he was primarily intending to rebut? Such arguments tend to be versions of what is called the argument from illusion, and run as follows. Even if there is such a thing as a state of perfect knowledge of the sort we have been talking about, there is an indistinguishable state in which things seem to us just the same, but are not in fact so. We cannot tell the difference between the two, though one is supposed to be knowledge-conferring and the other is definitely not so (since one cannot know something which is false). But if we cannot tell the difference between the two, how can the fact that we are in the better one suffice to give us knowledge? For all we know, we are in the other, mistaken, state. But how can we be said to know that there is a tree in front of us if for all we know there isn't?

There is a temptation to reply to this by citing further and extraneous facts, such as the fact that God is benevolent and that we know that this idea is caused by God, or the fact that we are normally right about what we think we see in front of us in broad daylight; and then to hope that these additions will justify us in saying that, though for all we know we might be wrong, still here we can count as knowing. But these responses admit something which Berkeley would dispute, which is that the perfect state might need some supplement before it can count as knowledge. They have reallowed something that Berkeley was hoping to rule out, namely the possibility that we are wrong; and hope to escape the consequences of this by showing that it is extremely improbable that we are. Berkeley would say that once the possibility of error is admitted, it is too late to hope to mend matters; for a perfect state is incompatible with the possibility of being mistaken.

The sceptical arguments try to drive a wedge between the state of having an idea of a real thing and knowing that you have an idea of a real thing. They urge that even if you are lucky enough to be in the former, you are never in the latter. You could, after all, mistakenly think that an idea of yours was caused in you by God. Otherwise none of us would ever be mistaken about whether an idea is part of a real thing. But this would be to go too far in the opposite direction. There are two dangers here. The first is to leave perceptual knowledge impossible, and the second is to leave hallucination impossible, i.e. to rule out the possibility that one thinks there are pink rats on the wall when there aren't. The only way to leave hallucination possible is to admit that we can be wrong about which of our ideas are caused in us by God. But once this is admitted, the wedge has been inserted between the state of having an idea of a real thing and knowing that one has an idea of a real thing.

How can Berkeley hope to avoid the insertion of this wedge? He would want to say that the distinction which the sceptic is trying to draw here is a distinction without a difference. There just is no room here for sceptical worry once we have grasped the notion of the perfect state which is identical with God's. For that state is one in which we are transparently locked onto a real thing; it just consists in having that thing before the mind. Once you are in that state, nothing further is required for you to know of its presence; and equally if you are not in that state, nothing further will suffice to get you into it. If you are in the perfect state, you need no supplement of the sort that the sceptic is trying to press upon you, and if you are not, no supplements will be any use to you.

Whether Berkeley's position here is in the end tenable or not, it offers a forthright and striking answer in an area which is still unresolved. And the answer offered is not available to Locke. But that does not mean that Berkeley's idealism is the only philosophy able to make this response to scepticism. It may still be possible for a realist of a non-Lockean sort to make similar moves.[3]

[3] Cf. J. McDowell 'Criteria, defeasibility and knowledge', *Proceedings of the British Academy* 1982, 68, pp. 455–79.

Direct realism

Locke's representative realism takes our perception of physical objects to be indirect; we see those objects in virtue of a more direct awareness of mental objects, ideas. There is a double awareness here, the two forms of which need to be marked by different names; we can say that we *see* physical objects and that we *perceive* ideas. This is called realism for obvious reasons, and representative realism because the ideas represent the physical objects to us. The full representative realist view, as we saw in chapter 1, is that we see an object when that object causes in us an idea which resembles it.

I have already stressed that this is a theory under which we do genuinely see physical objects and are not reduced to inferring their presence from the nature of our ideas. The latter view, which we called inferential realism, really deprives us of any *visual* contact with the outside world and turns the phenomenon of perception into some form of subconscious calculation. The representative realist wants to say that we have a genuine perceptual awareness of the world; our awareness of it is not quite the same as our awareness of ideas, but is analogous to it in some way that enables us still to think of both awarenesses as perceptual. But one of the pressures leading philosophers to adopt inferential realism is the thought that ideas and physical objects are such completely different sorts of thing that it is hard to make much sense of the claim that there are two different but analogous forms of awareness, one for each. Surely whatever awareness of physical objects is like, it can't be much like our direct awareness of our own ideas, not because it won't be direct (which is already agreed) but because our awareness of our ideas seems to be a very peculiar relation of which we can't conceive of there being a watered-down but still analogous version at all. How could physical objects be simply spread out for us in anything like the way that our ideas are?

Someone who is impressed by this sort of approach abandons representative realism, which is committed to the existence of an indirect form of perceptual awareness. But he has implicitly accepted the first move in representative realism, the view that we are directly aware only of our own ideas; his thought was only that there is no other form of awareness, and that our knowledge of the physical world is just not sufficiently similar to count as an indirect version of this one. But the main alternative position in the philosophy of perception is not this, but a theory which holds our awareness of the physical world to be direct. This theory, normally called direct realism (sometimes, not very politely, naïve realism), denies that our awareness of physical objects exists in virtue of a more direct awareness of ideas. Instead, it holds that we can achieve a direct perceptual contact with physical objects which is unmediated by an awareness of ideas or other mental objects.

The direct realist is like the inferential realist in being influenced by the thought that the notion of a double awareness is a fiction, but he takes the opposite route subsequently. Inferential theorists do without the second awareness, that of the physical; direct realists do without the first, that of the mental. In doing so they escape some of the inferential realist's objections to representative realism. The question whether we can really conceive of the physical world being spread out for us to see in anything like the way our ideas are simply fails to get a bite. But other difficulties remain. Can we make good sense of the claim that in *seeing* physical objects we are in direct perceptual contact with them? There are three sorts of reasons standardly produced for rejecting this claim. First is the fact that we sometimes make perceptual errors. How is this possible if our contact with the perceived world is so direct? Second is the thought that we simply cannot be in direct contact with something that is at a distance from us. There are two versions of this question, spatial and temporal. First it may be asked how I can be directly aware of objects that are miles away from me, and second how I can be directly aware of objects that have ceased to exist by the time that I become aware of them. The latter question is sometimes called the time-lag argument; the sort of case that raises the difficulty is the case of a distant star that has exploded by the time we on earth become able to see it. Third is the thought that recent advances in neuroscience reveal enormous complexity in the mechanism of perception, and therefore that however the common man may conceive of the matter, scientists know that our perception of physical things is far from direct, since it is mediated by activity in the visual cortex etc. etc..

The direct realist, if he has any sense, will be unmoved by these attacks. All that is needed to see this is to remember what he meant by saying that perception is direct awareness of a physical world. What was meant by this was that we are aware of the world, and our awareness of it is not mediated by or does not exist in virtue of an awareness of any intermediary object. This being so, the intermediary stages discovered by modern neuroscience do not constitute an objection to direct realism, since the objects concerned are not objects of which we are aware; *a fortiori*, then, they are not intermediate objects of awareness, and so their existence is not the sort of thing that direct realism is denying. Nor does the direct realist hold that direct awareness is direct in the sense that touch is direct, i.e. that all sensing is done by direct contact; the notion of visual contact, which I have been using above, is not to be taken literally. So there can perfectly well be direct awareness of objects at a distance from us. Nor is there any reason why the lack of an intermediary should be more puzzling once we recognise the time-lag caused by the fact that light does not travel at infinite velocity. The question whether there is a time-lag and the question whether there is an intermediary just seem to be two different questions.

What about the question how it would be possible for us to make mistakes about the things we see if we were directly aware of them and of their nature? The direct realist can make either of two moves here. The first is simply to repeat his definition of 'direct' and to point out that it just does not follow from this that the objects we are directly aware of must be in every respect the way we take them to be. Direct awareness need not be infallible awareness. The second, more congenial to our discussion in this chapter, is to accept that anything of which one is directly aware must be as it seems to one to be, but to claim that there is another state which we can easily confuse with that of direct awareness, but which is in fact very different. When we are directly aware of the blueness of an object, the object must indeed be blue. But there is another and less desirable state, easily confused with the first, which is one in which an object merely seems to be blue. There may in some cases be no recognisable differences between the two states, so far as their owners are concerned. But there is a huge difference in fact. One is conceived as a kind of openness to a state of affairs, an openness which could not exist if the state of affairs did not exist. The other is an opaque state of ourselves, about which the nature of the world around us has nothing to say.

Direct realists can choose between these options, then. And this means that there is a form of realism which bids fair to enjoy all the epistemological advantages that could be claimed for Berkeley. The second option is just Berkeley's theory of perception adapted for a realist point of view. And it seems to make available the same response to sceptical arguments.

Direct realism of this sort is just like Berkeley's idealism in that it inserts no gap between us and the world we live in and perceive. We are not in the position of having to look behind appearances in order to discern reality. Appearances simply are reality, most of the time; the way things look is the way they are. Perception takes place when surrounding objects impress their existence and nature upon us. And this explains why direct realists, like Berkeley, take experience seriously; they are unwilling to discount or treat as a distortion any of the ways in which objects appear to us, because of their general view that objects appear to us just as they are. Direct realists have to take their experience seriously because for them there is no filter through which objects appear to us, or by which reality is turned into appearance. It is in this sense that direct realism offers realists a new and promising account of the old contrast between appearance and reality, errors about which are the source of a great deal of bad philosophy.

With this in hand, we can return to Berkeley. Berkeley is not a realist, but it is tempting to say that he agrees with the direct realist about the directness of our perception of the physical world, and with the indirect or representative realist that the immediate objects of perception are mental objects; and that he thereby succeeds in getting the best of both worlds. There is truth in this, but any similarity between Berkeley and representative realists derives entirely from his view that physical objects are mental objects, ideas of sense. Berkeley's theory of perception is that it is a direct rather than an indirect relation between the mind and the physical world. And he takes this to be a major advantage of his position, for it enables him not only to make sense of but to endorse as exactly right the common sense view that the world we live in is the world we see. Berkeley would claim that this is a strength of his theory, and that it is a strength which his opponents cannot share. The first part of this seems correct; here Berkeley is in agreement with common sense, and he is going to use that fact for all it is worth. But the second part depends on who his opponents are. If the opponent is the representative realist, he is right. But what if the opponent is the direct realist, that is, a non-Lockean realist who takes it that we have direct awareness of a non-mental physical world? Such a person shares the advantage Berkeley claims for himself, that the world we live in is one of which we are directly aware. And he shares also any advantages in the fight against scepticism. Berkeley did not see these points, because he did not see the possibility of a realist version of his direct theory of perception. But is there any other advantage that he could claim, which would distinguish his directness theory from its realist rival?

I see two possible advantages for Berkeley here. The first derives from a question we raised earlier. The difference between Berkeley and his realist rival lies in the way they conceive of the other end of the perceptual relation. The realist holds that this is an irreducibly physical, non-mental thing. But I think that Berkeley would try to argue that this conception of the physical makes it very much harder to suppose that the mind can be directly related to it. The question earlier was how there could be such a relation between a mind and anything as foreign to it as the realist's physical objects. Mind and matter are two such disparate sorts of thing that though we may hopefully say that the one can be in direct touch (sorry) with the other, we cannot really do more than *say* this. We cannot construct a satisfying account of how this is possible. So if the mental and the physical are held distinct, as Berkeley's realist opponent would wish them to be, there seems to be little hope of a direct relation between them.

The second advantage I see for Berkeley lies in the problems raised for the realist by the distinction between primary and secondary qualities. Earlier we claimed that Locke's method of drawing this distinction, in terms of a resemblance or lack of it between physical objects and our ideas of them, collapsed into incoherence. Our ideas do not resemble physical objects in respect of their primary qualities, since ideas have no shape or size, and though they may change they do not move. It was if anything more promising to suppose that our ideas of the secondary qualities might resemble those qualities as they are in the object, though this would not be something Locke would wish to allow. But this is not the end of the story. First, Locke's version of the distinction is not the only possible one, even for a realist; Locke's realism is far from being the last word on the subject. But, second, no matter how we rewrite the distinction we are likely to find it in tension with the general thrust of direct realism. We have to be careful to ensure that any new version we adopt does not tend to lead us back to representative realism.

Why is the primary/secondary distinction likely to prove awkward for a direct realist? It is because any version of the distinction is likely to take our experience seriously only some of the time. We are going to find ourselves saying that the perception of the primary qualities is of a different order from that of the secondary ones, for the primary qualities are going to be allotted a different status in the objects that have them. Locke's account of that status was that only the primary qualities existed in the objects independent of any relation with a perceiving mind; the secondary qualities were seen only as powers or dispositions in the object to cause ideas in us, ideas which are not like those powers at all. A direct realist who adopted this position would be saying that though all perceivable properties are directly perceivable, it is only in the perception of some of them that we are discerning the independent nature of the physical world; in perceiving the others we are learning about that world only as it exists in relation to ourselves. But any position of this sort, no matter how its details go, is untrue to the way things seem to us as perceivers; it threatens to distort what is called the phenomenology of perception. The properties of physical objects are presented to us as all of a sort; the things we see seem to be independent possessors of colour, the things we feel seem to be independent possessors of heat, just as much as they seem to be independent possessors of shape and size. The appeal to the phenomenology of perception here is like Berkeley's appeal to common sense. For reasons given earlier, direct realists do make that appeal; and if they make it at all, they must make it consistently. So there is here a challenge to direct realism: see if you can write a distinction between primary and secondary qualities which remains consistent with the idea that all perception, that of colour as much as that of shape and size, is a direct awareness of an independent world.

The particular danger for a direct realist who wants to accept the primary/secondary distinction is that in trying to avoid saying that the colours we see belong to physical objects he may find himself attributing them to mental objects instead. For surely colour is directly perceived if anything is, and the colours we see need something to belong to. So if the physical objects are not themselves coloured, we may find ourselves admitting the existence of some other probably intermediate object which is coloured. But if this new object is an idea, we are back to representative realism, and once we have gone this far for colours, we might as well abandon direct realism altogether.

Our task now is to consider more recent versions of the distinction to see how well they meet this challenge. To do this we need to be clear about what the challenge is. To meet it we don't have to show that colour and other secondary qualities are in all respects like shape, size and other primary qualities. There will of course be differences between colour and shape. The challenge is to erect on those differences a general theory of the distinction between the primary and the secondary qualities which grants properties of the two sorts different status in our account of the physical world while retaining as much as possible of the common man's naïve belief that both are independent features of the experienced world.

Primary and secondary qualities

One differentiating feature of the primary qualities is that they all seem to be discernible by more than one sense: in fact by touch and one other sense. But nothing seems to emerge from this, for two reasons. The first is that it has no consequences for how we should conceive of the primary or the secondary. A property which is discernible by only one sense is not for that reason less securely placed within the independent world than is one that can be discerned by more than one sense; though mistakes about such a property might be less pervasive and less damaging to our expectations elsewhere than mistakes about a multiply perceivable property. Second, Berkeley would not have accepted the suggestion that different senses could discern the same property. For him an object is a collection of ideas, and the properties of objects are the ideas so collected. If properties are ideas, can the same idea be the product of more than one sense? Berkeley denied that there are in this way 'common sensibles'. This doctrine is expounded in his first published work, *An Essay towards a New Theory of Vision* (1709), where he wrote:

The extension, figures, and motions perceived by sight are specifically distinct from the ideas of touch called by the same names, nor is there any such thing as one idea or kind of idea common to both senses. (section 127)

Subsequent sections contain a defence of this claim, but the basic idea is an appeal to intuition. We are simply asked to reflect upon the nature of our own ideas, and we will easily accept that the idea we receive when we touch a square object is just not of the same sort as that received when we see a square object. Nor are we able to create for ourselves, perhaps by abstraction, an idea of squareness as a property which is discernible by several senses. It is true that we use the one word 'square' to denote ideas of several senses. But Berkeley insists that this is not because there is any real resemblance between those ideas; the explanation is rather that the different ideas are regularly available together, so that one is a sign of the other. This is our reason for packaging two ideas together under one name.

The idea that primary qualities are discernible by more than one sense does nothing to help us construct a revised version of the primary/ secondary distinction. But there is a second, more recent version, found perhaps first in Thomas Reid and recently revived by Gareth Evans,[4] which attempts to start from the claim that secondary qualities are related to experience in a way that primary qualities are not. Evans accepts the essence of Locke's account of the secondary; secondary qualities are dispositions in the objects to cause certain experiences in perceivers. The occurrence of those experiences is both necessary and sufficient for us to form the concepts of colour, sound, taste and so on. The difference between the primary and the secondary is, however, that while the secondary ones do not really figure in an interconnected theory of the world, the primary ones do. Indeed, as Evans writes:

The way these properties relate to experience is quite different from the way sensory properties relate to it. To grasp these primary properties, one must master a set of interconnected principles which make up an elementary theory – of primitive mechanics – into which these properties fit, and which alone gives them sense. One must grasp the idea of a unitary spatial framework in which both oneself and the bodies of which one has experience have a place, and through which they move continuously.[5]

The suggestion here is that experience is neither necessary nor sufficient

[4] See G. Evans 'Things without the mind', in Z. van Straaten (ed.) *Philosophical Subjects* (Oxford: Clarendon Press 1980), pt. 3.
[5] Ibid., p. 95.

for an understanding of the primary qualities, while the occurrence of the right sort of experience is both necessary and sufficient for an understanding of the secondary ones. Evans goes on:

The point is rather that it is not possible to distil the concept of hardness solely out of the experiences produced by deformation of the skin which is brought into contact with a hard object, for it is not possible to distil out of such an experience the theory into which the concept fits.[6]

Hardness, for Evans, is a primary quality because unlike qualities such as colour and taste we cannot really grasp the nature of hardness until we are in possession of something like a theory about the nature of the physical world. So the relation between experiences of hardness and the property of hardness is less direct than that between experiences of colour and the property of colour. Berkeley would have had none of this, because his extreme empiricism would have led him to deny the possibility of concepts whose connection with experience is as tenuous and indirect as this. For him, all concepts without exception would count as secondary, on the way Evans carves things up. But this does not in itself tell us whether this revised conception of the primary/secondary distinction succeeds in meeting the challenge made earlier. Does this account of the distinction, granting properties of the two sorts different status in our account of the physical world, succeed in retaining as much as possible of the naïve belief that both are independent features of the experienced world? Clearly it grants them different status; primary qualities can only be conceived within a general physical theory while secondary qualities, having a life of their own, seem not to be able to mesh into that theory at all. But what is the sense in which the secondary qualities are independent features of the experienced world? If they are conceived as independent of our experience of them, this can only be because they are independent of any particular experience. The essential relation between secondary qualities and experience is not denied, indeed is reinforced by calling them 'sensory'. This way of writing the primary/secondary distinction still conceives of the secondary qualities as concerned with the relation between the world and ourselves as perceivers, while the primary qualities are left able to be properties of a world independent of any such relation. In order to capture our sense that the secondary qualities are out there to be perceived, we have weakened the notion of independence at issue. There is a difference, then, between the independence of the primary qualities and that of the

[6] Ibid., p. 96.

secondary qualities. But perhaps this is only right and proper. We never insisted that the primary and the secondary be shown to be completely on a par.

The problem seems more to concern the sense which the new account gives to the idea of the experienceability of the secondary qualities. This is most easily seen with the example of colour. A coloured object is still conceived by Evans as one which has a power or disposition to cause certain experiences in us. A red object is one which has a disposition to cause a special sort of experience in a perceiver. It is true that our only method of saying what sort of experience is to use again the word 'red'. But there is no vicious circularity here. The difficulty concerns rather whether this account makes the required sense of our experience of colour. Does our experience represent coloured objects to us as ones which have dispositions to cause certain experiences? It seems manifestly that it does not. The colours of objects are experienced as non-dispositional properties, ways in which they simply are, not ways in which they are disposed to seem. So to believe the new account of the primary/secondary distinction we would have to accept that a large portion of our experience, that concerned with the secondary qualities, is not to be taken at face value. For our experience of colours represents them as non-dispositional when they are really dispositional.

The position then seems to be that though the new account may generate a satisfying conception of the primary qualities, it falls down when we come to the secondary ones. Can we perhaps improve matters by altering the account of the secondary while retaining the account of the primary untouched? The most natural way to move is to try to think of colour in the objects as the very same there as it seems to us to be; a red object is just the way it looks. But if we make this move, Berkeley can turn the tables against us, using our own stress on the sensory nature of the secondary qualities. A sensory quality is one which is essentially to do with experience, and this raises the question whether it is possible for a physical object to have a sensory property in this way. The matter seemed unproblematic enough while we were thinking of the secondary qualities as dispositions in the objects to cause certain experiences in us, dispositions which were grounded in the intrinsic primary qualities of those objects (even though we can perhaps never hope to explain how it is that objects of a certain sort come to look the way they do). But that easier conception did not make the required sense of our experience of secondary qualities, and we moved instead to a conception of the secondary qualities as existing in the objects somehow exactly as they do appear to us to be, rather than as faceless dispositions. But how can we make sense of the claim that an object which is in itself physical is able also to have qualities like this, qualities which need to be conceived in terms of the way they look or seem? Surely the intuition we were trying to capture was just that colour (like the other secondary qualities) is something to do with the way things *look* (or *seem*). Berkeley's idealism achieves this while his realist opponent cannot; there is no difficulty about conceiving of the secondary qualities as essentially to do with the ways things can look, because all properties are like that. Properties, in Berkeley's system, are ideas, and ideas are naturally to do with the ways things look or seem. On Berkeley's account of what it is for an object to be a physical object, there is no problem about supposing that such an object has among its properties some that concern the way it appears; the colour of an object is as much an idea of sense as is any other property of it.

There was another side to our intuition, the thought that colour is to do with the way things look in a way that the primary qualities are not. Here Berkeley does less well, because all properties are in principle alike for him. Though Berkeley is an idealist, he shares with the direct realist in the theory of perception a desire to think of perceiving as direct acquaintance with an independent world. Part of what is required in doing this is to make sense of our apparent ability to perceive an object as both round and red. Roundness and redness are here presented to us together, and presented in much the same sort of way; any differences between the perception of one and the perception of the other are very much matters of theory, not of experience itself. Berkeley's rejection of the primary/secondary distinction makes life easy for him here. It means that his theory fits experience perfectly, as of course it was designed to do. Against him we can perhaps say that his theory leaves colour and shape, or more generally the primary and the secondary, *too* undifferentiated. But the fact remains that we do not yet know how to do better, if we wish to retain the insights of direct realism. Berkeley's approach does seem to have, as he claimed, the advantage that it makes the best sense of our experience, even if his realist opponent would want to say that the loss of any primary/secondary distinction leaves him unable to show how colour (e.g.) is essentially to do with the way things look in a way that shape is not.

I said that Berkeley would claim two advantages over his realist rival, even where both think of perception as direct acquaintance with the world. The first was that it is easier to think of that acquaintance as direct if the world with which we are becoming acquainted is the idealist's world of ideas rather than the realist's stubbornly physical world. The second has been that the realist cannot find a satisfying conception of the secondary qualities. These hang uncomfortably in no man's land between us and the things we see; there is a tension within realism here between the desire to think of the secondary qualities as a facet of our the world and as a real property of physical objects, there to ced and existing in the objects just as they seem to us to be. In esolve this tension, realism oscillates violently between a ich distorts our experience of colour (for example) by saying that .... n colour is a disposition it is not experienced as a disposition, and a position which tries unsuccessfully to conceive of colour in the objects as a sort of objective seeming. Berkeley would argue that the latter is the only possible line, but that it is only available if we take the whole world as a sort of objective seeming, thinking of it as the ideas of sense.

In this chapter we have looked at Berkeley's claim that he is in a particularly good position to give an account of our knowledge of the world around us. We decided that his idealism offers a promising answer to sceptical attacks on the possibility of perceptual knowledge, but that there is a form of realism which gives the same answer. So we turned to his account of perception, and asked whether Berkeley was at an advantage in being able to conceive of perception as a direct relation between the perceiver and the objects he perceives. The answer again was that there is a realist position that enjoys any advantage that Berkeley can claim here. The last possibility was that Berkeley's account of our direct awareness of the world around us, and in particular his collapse of the distinction between primary and secondary qualities, made it possible for him to make good sense of the idea that our experience of colours and other secondary qualities is an experience of independent qualities of the objects we see. Here we did find something to be said for Berkeley, even though he only gained this advantage by considering all properties whatever as a form of objective appearance.

7

Science

The last chapter considered Berkeley's account of perceptual knowledge, and argued that he was able to offer a satisfying account of perception, and to make genuine headway against the sceptic who claims that perception cannot give us knowledge about the world around us. But there is another sort of knowledge that we have about that world, which is often contrasted with perceptual knowledge. This is scientific knowledge, knowledge generated by a successful and mature science. The sceptical argument we considered was as much directed against scientific knowledge as it was against perceptual knowledge, and more effective in this new area. The reason why scientific knowledge is vulnerable is that for us it seems irredeemably inferential; science surely always involves reasoning from what one sees to conclusions which go far beyond what anyone could hope to see. But God's knowledge of the facts that we know by inference is not inferential; it is direct. We are condemned to working out things that God knows straight off. This means that our state with respect to these things is never the most perfect possible, and never identical with God's; and so it cannot be true knowledge. But this is a most damaging conclusion for someone who, like Berkeley, saw contemporary science as offering the finest and best sort of human knowledge. Something had to be done, therefore, to preserve the claims of science.

As well as this problem about scientific knowledge, there is also one about scientific explanation. Berkeley was well aware that the realism which was his main target was closely associated with a philosophy of science, that is with an account of what science is doing and in particular of how scientific explanation works. He saw a danger that his readers would see the association, and conclude that to reject realism is to be unable to see any sense in natural science; and he was most anxious to rebut any such suggestion.

So Berkeley faces two difficulties in the attempt to give a satisfying account of science. That he feels the difficulties acutely may explain the somewhat defensive nature of his remarks about the philosophy of science. Symptomatic here is the fact that he buries them in that part of the *Principles* which he calls 'replies to objections'. We shall however conclude that he was wrong to be so comparatively diffident, and that his suggestions in (as he conceives it) his own defence are both novel and independently interesting. There are even reasons for seeing them as preferable to the theory he was attempting to supplant.

Whether this is so or not, Berkeley was peculiarly sensitive to the charge that his idealism rendered natural science redundant. The simplest way of making this objection is to say that if there is no physical world as conceived by science, there is surely nothing for science to investigate. But this conclusion had to be avoided at all costs, for two reasons. First, the investigations of scientists were beginning to show promise of improving the conditions of human existence, something of which pre-Enlightenment science seems to have been very short. Second and perhaps more important, there were the recent theoretical advances in science, notably the achievements of Newton. Berkeley had enormous admiration for Newton, thinking only that his realism was an unfortunate blemish (with also some later criticisms of Newtonian mathematics). In particular, the theoretical advances of Newtonian science bring an enormous and undeniable increase in the ability of science to explain natural phenomena. The first problem we shall consider for Berkeley is then how to retain a central place for science and its success in discovering new forms of explanation, without yielding to its tendencies towards realism.

Empiricism and realism

We may begin with a distinction between two classic positions in the philosophy of science, commonly called empiricism and realism. (Some-times empiricism is called instrumentalism, for reasons which will emerge shortly: it would be better to ignore for the moment the way we have used these labels earlier.) The empiricist holds that the purpose of science is to provide an explanation of the course of our experience. Science offers an apparatus of enormous power to do this; scientific explanations contain terms such as 'force' and 'atom', or in our own times 'proton', 'neutron', 'quark', 'positron' etc., and the role of these terms is to link together to form an explanatory language, competence with which can provide the sorts of explanation we are looking for. The realist holds, by contrast, that these terms are not just explanatory constructs. They name (or at least purport to name, and if our science is anywhere near correct do succeed in naming) discriminable parts of the world whose interactions generate the macroscopic events whose ex-planations we are seeking. For the realist, then, the theoretical terms of science name real, though unfamiliar, objects in the world. For the empiricist they do not, but serve purely as explanatory constructs whose purpose and justification lies in the need to make sense of our experience.

Locke was in these terms a realist. Although an empiricist in epistemology, holding that all our knowledge derives from our experience, he is not an empiricist in the philosophy of science. His position here is perfectly consistent; what is called empiricism in the philosophy of science is an extreme form of the general empiricist approach, which is to stress everywhere the sense in which we must start from our experience. As an extreme form, it holds that no term in science can name objects that lie beyond the reach of experience. But one doesn't need to be an extreme empiricist of this sort in science in order to be an empiricist in epistemology.

Locke's avoidance of the extreme position affects his account of scientific explanation. What is a scientific explanation of a natural event like, and why is it that such explanations do in fact succeed in explaining anything? For Locke, an explanation of an event must be *mechanical*. Locke sees physical objects as complex arrangements of invisible microscopic parts held together by some 'force'. How are we to think that change can occur in a world of such objects? Locke's answer is "by impulse, the only way we can conceive bodies operate in" (*Essay* 2.8.11). The explanation of any particular event, then, will involve finding its cause, and the cause will be whatever motion of bodies did in fact result in this event. If we can find an antecedent event suited for the causing of this event by the impulse of body on body or particle on particle, we have done all that we can in explaining it.

Why is it that such an explanation works? The answer to this question comes from considering the prime example of a mechanical explanation, namely the explanation of the motion of the hands of a clock in terms of the internal movements of its cogwheels. Causation in a clock works by impulse, that is to say by the different parts pushing each other about. We explain the motion of the hands by coming to see how the hands are driven by the spindle, which is driven by this wheel, which is driven by that wheel which is driven by a weight. And this procedure explains the motion of the hands because it restores our sense that, or leads us to see for the first time that, given the way the hands are linked to the mechanism the hands have *got* to move when the clock is wound. Mechanical explanation works because it leads us to see the event to be explained as necessary in the circumstances.

We might suppose that someone looking for the explanation of an event is someone for whom that event is or has become a mystery, someone who no longer sees any reason why that event should have occurred. A successful explanation will restore the sense that in those circumstances this event *should* have happened. But to see that it should have happened we need to see it as in fact required by the circumstances; this event couldn't help happening, given what happened just before. Mechanical explanation is powerful because it reveals a *necessary connexion* between this event and its antecedents, and in this way takes the mystery out of it.

Of course the mechanical aspect of the explanation is not the whole story. The mechanical story only works if we take it that the cogs are made of suitable metal, and the tensile strength and resistance of that metal, which we can think of as its general causal powers, will be expressed in a scientific law. Relevant laws are required, then, in addition to the specification of mechanical causes. But the explanations to which they contribute will only be successful if the whole story manages to restore our sense that the event to be explained was necessary in the circumstances, and this last is really the work of the mechanical side of the story. As Locke said:

> I doubt not but, if we could discover the figure, size, texture, and motion of the minute constituent parts of any two bodies, we should know without trial several of their operations one upon another, as we do now the properties of a square or a triangle . . . The dissolving of silver in *aqua fortis* and gold in *aqua regia*, and not *vice versa*, would be then perhaps no more difficult to know than it is to a smith to understand why the turning of one key will open a lock and not the turning of another. (*Essay* 4.3.25)

For Locke, then, it is impossible to explain an event without some appeal to regularities, an appeal which in a mature science surfaces as an explicit statement of the relevant scientific laws. But the purpose of that appeal, and the general aim of explanation, is to restore a sense of a necessary connexion between the event to be explained and the surrounding circumstances. Locke thought that, although we are completely unable to conceive what such necessary connexions might be like, we may be sure that they do exist. They are real features of the world, about whose presence we are reduced to an insecure and inferential knowledge.

In contrast to Locke, Berkeley is an empiricist in the philosophy of science. Terms in the language of science either name experienceable items or they name nothing and must play some other role than that of a name. The course of experience could not be explained by appeal to terms which name things which lie beyond experience, because for Berkeley there are no such things. The role of terms like 'mass' and 'energy' must then lie in the contribution such terms make to the explanation of experience, and such contribution must be of a completely different sort from that conceived in the mechanistic account of scientific explanation.

The problem for an empiricist such as Berkeley is then how to make good sense of the idea that the theoretical terms of science might make a contribution to the success of scientific explanation without doing this by naming microscopic items whose behaviour generates mechanically the events we are trying to explain. What is scientific explanation and how is it successful if it is not mechanical?

Regularity theories

The normal route for empiricist philosophies of science is to agree with Locke that regularities play an important part in scientific explanation, but to deny the real existence of necessary connexions between natural events: to deny, that is, the existence of what is called natural necessity. Explanation is achieved, not when we have begun to see the event to be explained as necessary in the circumstances, but rather when we have seen it as part of a larger pattern, a pattern expressed in a collection of scientific laws. So explanation is achieved, according to these empiricists, when we see how this event fits into a general structure of interconnected regularities expressed in scientific laws.

Does this mean that empiricism of this sort gives no sense to talk of necessary connexions between particular events? If it ruled out all talk of necessary connexions, and insisted that explanation simply involves finding a pattern within which this event fits, it would be offering a very thin account of scientific explanation. The suggestion would be that we have explained a phenomenon when we have placed it as part of some regular process or course of events. An event, on this approach, may strike us as odd or unusual, and so we seek an explanation for it. Our puzzlement is removed when we have come to see that it is not really odd or unusual at all, but perfectly normal. We see an event as normal when we have managed to subsume it under some true generalisation about the works of nature. And this is how scientific explanation, conceived as generalisation, succeeds in explaining.

Why is this account so thin? The simplest way to make the point is to say that it is not at all obvious why generalisation, conceived in this simple way, should ever succeed in removing the sense of mystery which we look to explanation to dissolve. For if I find some event or course of events mysterious, why should I be helped by being shown that the event or events are part of a regular pattern? All that this could do would be to increase my sense of mystery here rather than to reduce it. I might agree that the event is normal, without losing at all my sense that it is mysterious and that all the others like it are mysterious too; I emerge with two mysteries rather than one. I sought to dispel the sense of mystery by finding out *why* the event occurred, and this question does not seem to be answered at all by being told that it is part of a regular pattern. Of course I *might* be satisfied by this answer, but I shouldn't be. In consistency I should simply ask why there should be such a regular pattern. For scientific explanation is intended to provide *understanding* rather than acquiescence in place of puzzlement, and how have I been helped to understand an event merely by being told that it forms part of a regular pattern?

Sophisticated regularity theorists are well aware of this problem, of course. They deal with it by drawing a distinction between mere regularities, which are of no use in explanations, and scientific laws. The point is made by distinguishing between scientific law and accidental generalisations, or more generally between lawlike and accidental generalisations. The accidental generalisations are those universal truths which just happen to be true; the lawlike ones are generalisations which do not just happen to be true. For example, let us suppose that I order the books on my shelves alphabetically, and that it happens that all the books on one shelf have red covers. The statement that all the books on that shelf are red counts as an accidental generalisation. By contrast, the statement that all trees have leaves is, if true, not an accidental truth. Now the distinction between lawlike and accidental generalisation matters when it comes to the use of these universal truths in explanation. If I were to ask why some book on my shelf has a red cover, it would be no answer to say that all the books on that shelf are red, even though this is a true generalisation under which this book falls as an instance. If however I were to ask why that object has leaves, it would be (part of) an answer to say that it is a tree and all trees have leaves. The lawlike generalisation at least offers the beginnings of an explanation.

This difference between lawlike and accidental generalisation can be explained to some extent by noticing one particular differential feature of their logical behaviour. The statement

1   all the books on this shelf are red

does not imply

2   if that book were on this shelf, it would be red.

But the statement

3   all trees have leaves

does imply

4   if this were a tree, it would have leaves.

The difference here is often expressed by saying that lawlike generalisations imply subjunctive conditionals (statements of the form of 2 and 4), but accidental generalisations do not. How does this difference between two statements of apparently similar form (1 and 3) come about? The reason lies in the sort of statement being made. If it is merely accidental that all F things are also G, we will not be able to infer that if that thing, which is not F, had been F, it would have been G too. For the fact that all the things that are actually F are G is no reason to suppose that things in general have to be G if they are F. With a lawlike statement, such as 3, things are different. More is required for the truth of such a statement than just that all the actually F things should be G. And this means that the regularities that form part of successful explanations are not *mere* regularities, and so appeal to them can achieve more than showing that the event to be explained was normal, and so could have been expected in the circumstances. The mere fact that the generalisations with which we are here concerned are lawlike marks the difference between the regularities that explain and those that don't.

What has happened to the necessary connexions between particular events on this theory? There seem to be two possible answers to this question. The first is that there are no such things as links or ties between individual events for a regularity theorist. Events are not really interconnected in the sort of way that Locke seems to have thought that they were; there are however regular ways in which the natural world works, by appeal to which we can explain the occurrence of any event that puzzles us. This view roundly denies the existence of such a thing as natural necessity, of necessary connexions between events. For such a view, the subjunctive conditionals which carry the weight of any explanation are *barely* true; they are not made true by, or true in virtue of, some connexion between the events they describe. The truth that if this were a tree it would have leaves, for example, is not made true because there is a link in the natural world between being a tree and having leaves. There are no such links in nature, and explanation is not intended to restore our sense that there are. There is just the bare truth, which is still all we need for explanation, that if anything were a tree it would have leaves.

A realist would object to this that subjunctive conditionals cannot be barely true in this sort of way. They must be true because of something, and in this case the something is a natural link or necessary connexion between being a tree and having leaves. That link exists, and there isn't anything like it between being a book and being red; and that is why appeal to the subjunctive conditional seems to explain. It is because the subjunctive conditionals are only true when there are such necessary connexions in the world to make them true. A realist might even argue that not all subjunctive conditionals do have the sort of explanatory power that the regularity theorists ascribe to them, for some accidental generalisations can entail subjunctive conditionals. For instance, suppose that all my children are boys, and that I spy some child in the distance whose sex I cannot recognise. I might reasonably say that if that child were one of mine, it would be a boy. This seems to be a subjunctive conditional entailed by an accidental generalisation. And it reveals something that hitherto we perhaps only suspected, that the explanatory power of a subjunctive conditional, when it has it, is not something it has for itself but rather something which it borrows from something else. And of course the something else, for the realist, is just the existence of a necessary connexion in nature, a natural necessity, which makes the subjunctive conditional true.

I said, however, that there are two possible answers to the question I raised about what regularity theorists would say about these natural necessities. The first answer was to deny their existence (and probably even their conceivability). The second, more subtle, accepts that there are such things in a sense; but holds that their existence amounts to nothing more than the truth of the relevant subjunctive conditionals. There is a necessary connexion between being a tree and having leaves, but all that we mean by this is that if anything were a tree it would have leaves. The conditional here is barely true, but that does not mean that there are no natural necessities. There are natural necessities, but their existence simply consists in the truth of the relevant subjunctive conditionals. So this more subtle theory does not deny that there are links between events; instead, it gives its own account of what it is for there to be such links.

It might be helpful here to point out a similar stance in another area of philosophy. One traditional position in moral philosophy is to hold that there are no such things as moral properties in the natural world; actions are not really right or wrong. There only are attitudes of approval and disapproval, which are in us and not in the actions we approve of. A more subtle position is to hold that actions are right or wrong, but that all such a state of affairs amounts to is that we approve or disapprove of them. This view does not attempt to deny that actions have moral properties, but attempts merely to give its own account of what this amounts to.

Returning to the philosophy of science, we can see why the first sort of regularity theory should be called an anti-realist account of natural necessity (anti-realist now in the old sense of 'realist', not in the sense of the contrast between realist and empiricist in the philosophy of science). For it roundly asserts that natural necessities are not real; there are no real necessary connexions between natural events. But the second, more subtle theory is also anti-realist about natural necessity in its general thrust, though one can see why such theories have been called 'quasi-realist'.[1] They pretend to give the realist all he wants, or all he can reasonably want, and then somehow take it away again.

The simplest way to make this point is perhaps to return to moral philosophy. What has the realist about moral properties lost if he moves instead to the more subtle form of anti-realism? The answer is, I think, that he begins to feel distanced from his own moral experience. We all know the phenomenon of seeing an action whose wrongness hits us in the face, as it were. But the anti-realist account of this cannot avoid alienating us from our experience, causing us to treat it as a situation where our autonomous rationality is somehow impugned. If we really believed the anti-realist story, our own cognitive states would begin to seem like alien intrusions.

The same seems to be true in the philosophy of science. On the subtler form of regularity theory, despite its apparently conciliatory remarks, it is going to be impossible to retain one's sense that there are necessary con-nexions between particular events. At the end of the day, both sorts of regularity theory are anti-realist about necessary connexions. Whether there is a necessary connexion here has become a matter of what can reasonably be inferred from what, and the question whether in drawing those inferences we are really following a path that the world follows too has somehow disappeared.

So far we have been stressing the anti-realist nature of regularity theories, and have mentioned one difficulty for them. This was the thought that appeal to subjunctive conditionals may not really suffice to ground the distinction which they need between lawlike and accidental generalisations. One further difficulty may be mentioned. This is that theories of this sort are hard put to make good sense of the hope that a science which is explanatorily successful will be the truth. For it seems that, even if we were lucky enough to find one such theory, there is always the possibility of another one, equally good but different. Some philosophers would go so far as to claim that we know in advance that there will be such a thing. For a scientific theory, on this approach, is just

[1] See S. Blackburn *Spreading The Word* (Oxford: Clarendon Press 1984), ch. 6, esp. sec. 5.

a tool whose whole value lies in its ability to explain. It is not an attempt to deliver the truth about the natural world, and should not be judged as if it were. For regularity theorists, and for empiricists in general, then, science is indeterminate. There is no suggestion that our science, or any other science, is or could be uniquely the truth. And this counts as a difficulty because it is, at least to some extent, counter-intuitive. We do feel that there are facts of the matter here, some of which our science has already succeeded in capturing, and empiricist theories of science are in danger of undermining this feeling.

Berkeley's account

We have seen two rival philosophies of science, and two accounts of scientific explanation. Where does Berkeley come in all this? Unfortunately neither of the positions we have outlined is available to him. Locke's position is impossible for him for two reasons. The first is that the necessary connexions of which Locke speaks emerge only from a mechanist conception of the intricacy in the natural world. Take away the mechanism, and the necessary connexions vanish as well. But there is a second difficulty for Berkeley too. This is that the connexions as Locke saw them were causal connexions, and Berkeley gives no sense to the notion of a causal connexion between natural events. For him, natural events are ideas of God's, and since ideas are passive no idea can be the cause of any other idea, for only active things (minds) can cause:

A little attention will discover to us that the very being of an idea implies passiveness and inertness in it, insomuch that it is impossible for an idea to do any thing, or, strictly speaking, to be the cause of any thing. (P. 25)

At this point in the *Principles* Berkeley is arguing that since the properties of objects are only ideas, and ideas cannot be causes, our ideas of objects cannot be caused by any properties of those objects, but must be caused by something active, viz. a mind. He is swinging into his causal argument for the existence of God. For our purposes the point is that the entities discovered by science are still ideas, for Berkeley, and that therefore we can make no sense of the mechanist claim that the operations of these entities function as causes of natural events. But there are two ways we could take the thought that ideas cannot be causes. The weak way would be to say that ideas, being passive, cannot initiate causal chains of events. We could say this on the analogy of something admittedly passive such as a hammer. Hammers cannot initiate causal changes, but the motion of a hammer can transmit causal change. In this sense hammers can be intermediary causes, and ideas can do this as well. The only initiating causes will be minds, but those minds can use their ideas as tools to cause the occurrence of other ideas. A stronger position would however be that ideas cannot be used as tools in this way at all, i.e. that they can be neither initiating nor intermediary causes. Someone might be tempted to adopt this stronger position because he could not see how an idea, or the occurrence of an idea, could transmit agency of any sort.

Berkeley must, I think, take the stronger of these two positions. But its inevitable result is that the microscopic events are not events that God could use to cause other ideas in us. They cannot be causes of anything, and so the whole purpose of the intricate detail that science is discovering in the natural world becomes entirely mysterious.

If Locke's position is (unsurprisingly) not available to him, could Berkeley adopt a regularity theory instead? Sadly, this option too is ruled out for him. This is because he is not in a position to accept the anti-realist approach to the existence or otherwise of necessary connexions. Berkeley, we should remember, shares with realists, particularly direct realists, the inclination to take our experience of the world as seriously as possible. This is not just because our experiences are the gift of God, and we should be very careful before discounting such gifts as not genuinely representing the way the world is. More to the point is the fact that if we have an idea that comes from God, which indeed we share with God, there is no possibility that the idea be not (part of) a real thing. For the ideas that are (part of) real things are just those which enjoy the right degree of independence from us. Now the distinctive feature of a sophisticated regularity theorist is just his anti-realism about necessary connexions between natural events: about natural necessity. Berkeley would remember that we do experience natural events *as* necessarily connected, some of the time. Causation *seems* to be a real relation between real events; we find it very hard to give up the thought that it is possible for one event actually to *make* another happen. But the anti-realists are discounting these appearances in a way which for Berkeley involves ignoring things which are definitely real. So the sort of anti-realism that is associated with a regularity theory is not possible for Berkeley.

This seems to leave Berkeley in a very awkward position, where neither of the leading accounts of scientific explanation is within his reach. His eventual response is to provide something completely different from either of them. But we need first to follow him along the path a little. His first suggestion in the *Principles* is that we explain an event by showing that it is part of the regular order of things: that is, by showing

that it falls under a true generalisation about the ideas of sense. He
writes:

There are certain general laws that run through the whole chain of natural
effects: these are learned by the observation and study of nature, and are by men
applied . . . to the explaining the various *phenomena*: which explication consists
only in showing the conformity any particular phenomenon hath to the general
laws of nature, or, which is the same thing, in discovering the *uniformity* there is
in the production of natural effects. (P. 62)

He gives slightly more detail in *Principles* 105:

If therefore we consider the difference there is betwixt natural philosophers [i.e.
scientists] and other men, with regard to their knowledge of the *phenomena*, we
shall find it consists, not in an exacter knowledge of the efficient cause that
produces them, for that can be no other than the *will of a spirit*, but only in a
greater largeness of comprehension, whereby analogies, harmonies, and agreements are discovered in the works of nature, and the particular effects explained,
that is, reduced to general rules.

In saying that the explanation of an event is merely its reduction to
general rules, Berkeley looks as if he is providing a very simple account
which pays no attention to the important distinction between lawlike and
merely accidental generalisation, and hence does not tell us why
subsumption under law succeeds in being explanatory. But Berkeley
does have a way of joining the sophisticated regularity theorist in
distinguishing between lawlike and accidental generalisations, thus:

Now the set rules or established methods, wherein the mind we depend on
excites in us the ideas of sense, are called the *laws of nature* (P. 30)

The idea here is that there may be some regularities in our experience
which are accidental, i.e. unintended by God, and others which are the
regularities which God imposes on the ideas of sense. If there were such
a difference, statements about the regularities imposed by God would
imply subjunctive conditionals just as our scientific laws do, and the
merely accidental regularities would not. So this Berkeleian addition is
some advance. In Berkeley's system God's benevolence, i.e. his deter-
mination to work in a predictable way, would generate a workable
distinction between those generalisations which imply subjunctive conditionals and those which don't. This is true, at least, so long as we can
distinguish between those features of the natural world which God
intends and those which he does not.

We have already floated the idea that the subjunctive conditionals, important though they are, play their role in explanation only because their truth shows us that there must be some necessary connexion in virtue of which they are true; it is the necessary connexion that we are really after, and which the explanation is intended to reveal. A barely true subjunctive conditional would not provide a genuine explanation, and some subjunctive conditionals emerge from accidental regularities, and so do not offer explanations at all. The same point now arises for Berkeley, but in a different way. Although he is in a position to provide his own version of the distinction between accidental and lawlike generalisations, by showing that the one do and the other do not imply subjunctive conditionals, it is not really the subjunctive conditionals we are after, but the sense of necessity which they express. And Berkeley's way of generating them does nothing to restore our sense of necessity; we do not regain our sense that particular events in the natural world are linked by any sort of necessity, so that if the first happens the second is somehow compelled to happen as well. We can know now what God will do, i.e. what to expect in the physical world. But we can have no sense of *why* things should go this way. All we can do is to take it that they will. But if we can only predict what will happen without any understanding of why it should, surely we are still left without an explanation of our experience. We said at the beginning that an appeal to merely accidental regularities fails to provide an understanding of why a natural event occurred, even though it might enable us to predict that event with success. And it seems that this is still true despite the detour through God.

The question still is what Berkeley can put in place of the mechanist's sense of a necessity or inexorability that links different events in the physical world. That notion was derived from the inexorability of the intricate workings of a machine, and this in itself explained the fact that the physical does contain the intricacy that physics reveals. The intricate workings are required because that is the only way in which the machine, conceived of mechanically, could get to operate. But for Berkeley the intricacy seems redundant. If the laws of nature, i.e. the regularities with which God operates in providing the ideas of sense, do revolve around this sort of intricacy, why should this be? Has God just decided to make things difficult and expensive for us to unravel? And can nothing be said about why God should make such a choice? Surely we should not be in the business of supposing that God makes important choices of this sort for no real reason at all, and yet this seems to be the consequence of Berkeley's views so far.

Berkeley puts the point in this way:

In short, it will be asked, how upon our principles any tolerable account can be given, or any final cause assigned of an innumerable multitude of bodies and machines framed with the most exquisite art, which in the common philosophy have very apposite uses assigned them, and serve to explain abundance of phenomena. (P. 60)

And he continues:

ideas are not any how and at random produced, there being a certain order and connexion between them, like to that of cause and effect: there are also several combinations of them, made in a very regular and artificial manner, which seem like so many instruments in the hand of nature, that being hid as it were behind the scenes, have a secret operation in producing those appearances which are seen on the theatre of the world, being themselves discernible only to the curious eye of the philosopher [i.e. scientist]. But since one idea cannot be the cause of another, to what purpose is that connexion? and since those instruments, being barely *inefficacious perceptions* in the mind, are not subservient to the production of natural effects; it is demanded why they are made, or, in other words, what reason can be assigned why God should make us, upon a close inspection into his works, behold so great variety of ideas, so artfully laid together, and so much according to rule; it not being credible, that he would be at the expense (if one may so speak) of all that art and regularity to no purpose? (P. 64)

There are two questions, then. First, why should God choose one set of regularities rather than another? Surely without a reason for his choice, it is accidental; and our ability to know what rules God has accepted and hence to predict the future is not accompanied by an ability to *understand why* things should have been chosen to happen this way. The world and its order remains stubbornly accidental, and therefore incomprehensible. We never regain our sense of a necessary connexion between distinct events. Second, what is the point of all the intricacy? Why did God choose to frame his regularities in this artful and complicated way? The intricacy is not necessary to God as a means or tool, for God has no need of any intermediary or tool. So what is the point of it? It looks at this stage as if Berkeley has no answer to these complaints. Everything he has to say in the *Principles* about regularities and God's benevolence leaves him wide open to this sort of attack.

His version of the regularity theory is also in difficulty when it comes to making sense of science's claim to provide not just an explanation, nor even a successful explanation, but the *right* explanation of changes in nature. Physics claikms to tell us the truth, or at least to be well on the way to telling us the truth. But this claim is not one of which Berkeley can make much sense. So far as we can yet see, any theory which successfully passes the only test, which is whether it can generate the right predictions, is as good as any other; and there is no reason why there should not be several such theories, so long as we distinguish theories not only by the predictions they make but also by their internal machinery, i.e. the way in which the theory works to yield the prediction.

But there remains one strand of Berkeleian thought in this area which we have not tapped. For it is at this point that Berkeley introduces his most distinctive and interesting thought in the philosophy of science. This is the fascinating idea that the intricate workings of the world of sense are to be compared with the intricate workings of a language, and understood and explained on the analogy of a language, one in which God is speaking to us. It is round this revolutionary suggestion that Berkeley builds a new and different account of science.

The linguistic analogy

The *Principles* contain the rudiments of an account of natural science as the attempt to learn the language in which God is speaking to us. Individual events are conceived on this account as utterances of God's, our understanding of which is to be taken on the model of our understanding of ordinary utterances, so that to understand an event will be to know what it means.

Berkeley starts by suggesting that the different events in the world do not occur entirely unrelated to each other, but neither are they related causally; for one idea cannot cause another. Instead, one idea is the *sign* of another:

The connexion of ideas does not imply the relation of *cause* and *effect*, but only of a mark or *sign* with the thing *signified*. The fire which I see is not the cause of the pain I suffer upon my approaching it, but the mark that forewarns me of it. (P. 65)

With this altered conception of the relations between ideas, he is able to swing into his account of the intricacy of the world. The idea here is that different events form signs, and these signs are part of a system of signs or language. The language is one in which God is giving us notice of the future. His infinite benevolence causes him to make it possible for us to come to understand the language he is talking here and hence act for our own preservation and comfort. And natural science is just the systematic attempt to come to know the language of God:

And it is the searching after, and endeavouring to understand those signs instituted by the author of nature, that ought to be the employment of the natural philosopher, and not the pretending to explain things by corporeal causes; which doctrine seems to have too much estranged the minds of men from that active principle, that supreme and wise spirit, *in whom we live, move, and have our being.* (P. 66)

If the experienced world constitutes a series of language-like utterances of God's, which we can come to understand in the way in which we understand human utterances and language, we have found yet another sense in which Berkeley's God is far closer to us in our ordinary experience of the world than as conceived in ordinary religious belief. And the analogy between world and language turns out to contain surprising richness, for Berkeley is able to give a new and original account of the intricacy of the ideas of sense by appeal to it:

The reason why ideas are formed into machines, that is, artificial and regular combinations, is the same with that for combining letters into words. That a few original ideas may be made to signify a great number of effects and actions, it is necessary they be variously combined together: and to the end their use be permanent and universal, these combinations must be made by *rule*, and with *wise contrivance.* (P. 65)

Why is there so much detail in the world if God had no need of such detail in order to achieve the regularities there that help us run our lives with safety and comfort? The answer lies in the thought that if the passing show of the ideas of sense constitutes a series of utterances, the ideas of sense must contain sufficient complexity to enable every significant difference in the thing signified to be captured by a difference in the sign. Language is like this; although there is only a finite number of words and constructions in English, the language can be used to say an infinite number of different things. Berkeley's thought is that though there are only a small number of different elements in the ideas of sense, corresponding to the proper objects of the five senses, these different elements can be put together in an infinite number of different ways. And the only way we have to make sense of this is to conceive of the relation between the paucity of material and the variety of message on the analogy of that between the limited basic elements of language and the infinitely various things that language can be used to say.

Our first task in investigating the strength of this analogy is to decide exactly what Berkeley is thinking of as the elements of language. This is because the general intention of the analogy is to explain the complexity and orderliness of the world by seeing it as analogous to the complexity and orderliness of a language. Berkeley's only specific suggestion has already been mentioned; it is that the elements are the letters, from different combinations of which we can construct enormous numbers of different words. But this is surely the wrong way to do it. For the ability of a finite language to represent an infinite number of different states of affairs is not dependent upon its being like English, and particularly not on its being like *written* English. It is true that we have devised a way of writing any English word in a system consisting of only 26 letters. But this fact is not particularly significant. First, those who can neither read nor write may still understand utterances in English perfectly well, despite their inability to think of the different words as composed of letters and their ignorance of how this sort of composition works. And this would mean, if we follow the analogy through, that scientific knowledge is dispensable. For the best possible understanding of events in the natural world would be available to people who knew nothing of science. Second, Berkeley rightly wants to stress as a feature of his analogy the thought that the natural world needs rules just as language does. In *Principles* 65, quoted above, his thought seems to be that unless the combinations of parts into wholes be regular, i.e. governed by rule, the utterances of God will be incomprehensible to us. This is an important part of what he wants to say, but it does not fit the idea that the basic elements of God's language here are to be conceived of on the analogy with letters. For letters are not combined to form words by rules. There are no rules for the formation of words out of letters at all. Berkeley needs to say that there are, because he wants to find some analogy within his model of language for the laws of science. The laws of science express general ways in which things work, but there do not seem to be any general rules for the combination of letters into words at all.

In general we must distinguish two sorts of linguistic complexity, the syntactic and the semantic. (Berkeley is using a syntactic complexity to explain a semantic one.) The syntax of English concerns the way in which we can combine words of different sorts to make English sentences. The semantics of English concerns the way in which words with different sorts of meanings can be combined to yield one thought, and what the meaning of that thought is, i.e. how it relates to the world. These two concerns are obviously related, but they are nonetheless distinct. Berkeley's thought is that if God's messages are to be able to represent as distinct an infinite number of different states of affairs, there must be somehow available an infinite number of different messages. And if we as God's audience are to be expected to understand all the different things that God is or may be saying to us, we must be in command of a way of decomposing the different messages into their component parts and the ways in which those parts are put together in each case. He thinks of this skill, correctly, as like the skill of someone competent with a language; and, incorrectly, as like the skill of someone who knows the rules that govern the ways in which the different letters are used to construct words in a written language. It would have been better to have concentrated instead on the way in which meaningful parts (words, or meaningful parts of words) can be combined into meaningful wholes (statements).

Once this point is sorted out it becomes possible to see that Berkeley's account of science as the attempt to learn the language of God is enormously suggestive, and offers a rich and promising philosophy of science which generates far better answers to questions about the relation between scientific and non-scientific knowledge and to many other difficult problems about science. Berkeley's views here have been inexplicably neglected, partly perhaps because the *Principles* as we have them contain only a few hints which need to be teased out. But I want to suggest that they are a rich and untapped source of good philosophy of science, and also that they constitute an important move in the progress of eighteenth-century thought. This claim is the subject of the next chapter.

In this chapter we have seen how mechanical explanation can restore our sense that the event explained was necessary, i.e. had to happen, in the circumstances. Berkeley's first account of explanation as generalisation failed in this respect, and so did the elaboration of it which distinguished between accidental and lawlike generalisations by appeal to the intentions of God. The analogy between linguistic understanding and scientific explanation is already proving more promising.

8

The Language of God

What sort of knowledge is scientific knowledge? What Berkeley wants to say is that the ordinary man can indeed hope to be in a position to interpret, with some degree of accuracy, the utterances of God; but the scientist can do it better. Scientific knowledge has to be conceived of as extremely helpful but not exactly essential, since God's language is one which all can understand but which the scientist can somehow understand better. Ordinarily the scientist is thought of as someone whose main distinguishing advantage is that he knows the causes and effects of natural events; he knows why things happen and what will happen after them. Berkeley's way of making sense of this is to say that the scientist understands better the meaning of each individual event, conceived as a linguistic occurrence. Does this leave us with a promising account of the relation between scientific and ordinary knowledge?

Let us take as our example the contrast between the ordinary and the scientific knowledge of the weather. All of us, after reasonable experience, are able to predict the weather with moderate success. Our knowledge here is based on our experience, and the experience is experience of regularities. But the regularities concerned are comparatively crude ones, and our success in extracting from them anything in the way of reliable and detailed knowledge of tomorrow's weather is accordingly limited. Scientific study of the weather reveals to us far more in the way of regularities; it both improves on and to some extent replaces the everyday knowledge of the common man. In this sort of way it tells us more, but only more of broadly the same sort of thing. This is Berkeley's position. The question then becomes why God could not have achieved his purposes here without resorting to the sort of intricacy that science discovers. And the answer is that without this intricacy only very limited information could be extracted from the regularities available to common experience. God therefore could only achieve his end of making available to us the maximum amount of information if he took the course we know him to have taken.

Where does the analogy with language come into all this? First we learn that each event is a sign to us of those with which events of that sort are regularly connected. But how does the idea that we should see these signs as part of a language-like system improve the situation? Perhaps the contrast between human language and birdsong tells us what is at issue here. Each species of bird has a limited range of different songs, each of which is correlated with one broad sort of situation. What can be done to improve the birdsong language, to enable it to impart more information to its users? The only thing that can be done is to add further tunes to it, and since each tune is as far as we can tell an indivisible unit, we cannot move from our knowledge of the sense of one tune to the knowledge of that of any other, nor construct a significant new tune from different significant parts of old ones. No part of a tune contributes to the meaning of the whole in the way that a word contributes to the meaning of any sentence in which it appears. And it is in virtue of this difference that human language is such an enormously powerful conveyor of information. New infor-mation can be encoded and decoded using only old resources.

The suggestion here cannot be that we are like the birds and scientists like the humans in the above story; for this would leave ordinary language as non-compositional (i.e. as containing utterances which are not constructed from semantically significant parts), which it is not. Instead I think that the right analogy is between someone at an early stage of learning a language in practice, with no knowledge of grammatical theory, and someone who has the ordinary ability of a competent adult speaker to conceive of utterances, whether his own or those of others, as composed of different words, each of which plays its own role. One can start learning a language sentence by sentence, with no knowledge of how those sentences are divided up into words. The understanding we have at this stage is crude, especially because we have not yet acquired a means of coming to understand a new sentence on the basis of the ones we already know, by seeing it as constructed of parts with whose functions we are already acquainted elsewhere. But one can move from this crude understanding to the more sophisticated one without difficulty, provided that the language is itself constructed in the right sort of way.

The thought then is that the scientist is distinguished by his ability to decompose whole utterances into their component words. In this way I think we can make the best sense of Berkeley's attempt to understand the role of science and how it can add something important to an already functioning though crude method of understanding the world.

Now that we know what the subject matter of science is, we can begin to see Berkeley's answer to the problem raised in the last chapter about how science can hope to yield knowledge. The difficulty was that scientific knowledge seemed to be entirely inferential, while God's knowledge of the same facts was direct; and hence no matter how reliable the beliefs of scientists, they could never count as true and perfect knowledge. Berkeley's account of science as the attempt to learn God's language begins to dissolve this difficulty. Scientific knowledge is conceived of as continuous with our ordinary perceptual knowledge about the world around us; by beginning to understand the ways in which God's utterances are composed, science offers us something similar to but better than what we had already. In coming to understand better the nature of the events we see, our perceptual knowledge is broadened. Scientific knowledge is therefore an improved form of perceptual knowledge, and should not be thought of as distinct on the grounds that the one is inferential and the other is not. So the gap between our scientific knowledge and God's knowledge of the same facts diminishes, for Berkeley. Of course there is still a long way for us to go. God knows infinitely more about everything than we do. But his knowledge is now everywhere of the same type as a knowledge to which we can reasonably aspire. The gap between us has become one of degree rather than one of type. And we may hope that some of our knowledge at least will be just like God's; although God knows more, this need not mean that our knowledge of what we do know is doomed to be less perfect than God's. Berkeley's approach can reinstate, then, the claims of science to generate knowledge.

Natural and non-natural meaning

We now return to the question raised in the last chapter, to which we have as yet found no answer. If we do accept this Berkeleian account of the world of sense as God's language, how does this help us to make sense of the ability of science to *explain* natural events? The analogy offers a sense in which the scientist understands natural events best; those events are utterances, and the scientist knows their meaning best. In this sense he understands them, but this does not yet tell him *why* they happened; even though he knows what they mean, he does not understand them in the sense of knowing why they happened. How then has the analogy with language enriched our account of scientific explanation? We seem still to be stuck with the thought that at the end of the day explanation is generalisation. The fact that the generalisations concern the habits of God did not help us to restore the sense of necessity in the way that we expect a successful explanation to do. We did not recover the thought that one event could be related in a non-contingent way to another, so that if the first happens the second has got to happen. So what is the point of all this? The relation between sign and object signified still seems to be based on regularities, and every event in the world is still arbitrary, being only contingently related to others.

So far we have spoken about the meanings of events such as the weather without much curiosity about what this might amount to. But we can understand such talk better by using a distinction between natural and non-natural meaning. (Current use of these terms is due to H. P. Grice;[1] we will adopt them now and abandon them later.) We commonly ascribe meaning to the clouds, as when we say 'those clouds mean rain', or 'those spots mean measles'. Here we are thinking only that clouds like those are normally followed by rain, or that spots like these can be expected to be pursued by an illness of such and such a sort. Such thoughts can be captured in an account written entirely around regularities, and though someone may use them to predict rain or measles, this ability does not in itself generate an ability to explain why rain will occur. Such a person knows that it will, but cannot really say why. Weather of this sort has a *natural* meaning. But we also have a notion of non-natural meaning, which is what is at issue when we say 'those three rings on the bell mean that the bus will not stop here' or that those frantic gestures mean that there is danger ahead. It is difficult to give an exact account of the difference between natural and non-natural meaning, as one can see from Grice's efforts in his article 'Meaning'. The examples given are intended to help you to get a sense of the distinction, without helping you yet to specify what difference is at issue. But the crucial point is that linguistic meaning is non-natural, not natural.

Berkeley has often been taken to be trying, hopelessly, to write an account of the nature of scientific law which is concerned solely with regularities and which is therefore not improved by the detour via the idea that the world of sense is God's language, since the utterances in that language are conceived as having only natural meaning. This attempt is hopeless because natural meaning is analysable solely in terms of regular sequences of events, which remain stubbornly contingent. But surely it should be obvious that when Berkeley talks of natural events as God's signs he means to suggest that they are utterances and so that their meaning is non-natural. Someone who knows how to understand those utterances knows what they mean (non-naturally), and this is not now the same as knowing what sorts of events are regularly connected with them. Berkeley's signs are not useful clues, but genuine utterances.

So far we have seen two advantages in the suggestion that science is the attempt to learn God's language. The first was that it enabled Berkeley to give an idealist account of the intricacy of the natural world, and hence of the subject matter of science. The second was that he became able to show how science could reasonably claim to offer

[1] See H. P. Grice 'Meaning', *Philosophical Review*, 1957, 66, pp. 377–88.

knowledge about that world. The distinction between natural and non-natural meaning gives him a third advantage. For he now gains a sense in which the relations between distinct events are not purely contingent. For one event can *mean* that another will occur, in the same way that an utterance 'it will rain' means that it will rain. The black clouds are an utterance of God's, which speaks about the future (and about the past too). So there is a relation between the two events which is not merely contingent, although it is still arbitrary in the sense that God could have chosen to mean something else by utterances of this sort. The relation between the two events is one of semantic necessity, since the first means that the second will happen or has happened. In this way we find ourselves able to combine both arbitrariness and necessity in the link between the same two events.

The notion of semantic necessity is important here because we can use it to show how we can explain one event by appeal to another. To do this, we agreed, we would have to show not merely that events like the first are always followed by events like the second, but also why this was so. Thinking of the world as containing arbitrarily chosen regularities, we found ourselves deprived of any explanation of those regularities other than that these were the ones that God had chosen; we still could not say *why* he chose them, and felt that this deprived us of something we needed, some sense of the appropriateness of the second event to the first. But now that we are thinking of the first event as a statement by God to the effect that the second event will occur, we can offer a sense in which the two events fit each other. For one of them simply means that the other will occur. Given this, if one has happened we can see a reason why the other one should, a reason which does not reduce to the thought that such events have occurred in regular relations in the past. The only additional element required for the explanation to go through is God's benevolence, i.e. that he is not a liar. But this is given at the beginning.

Of course it is still the case, on this account, that God's choices are arbitrary. But this need no longer disturb us. What we are learning is that our sense of there being necessary connexions between events can co-exist with a recognition that the whole pattern of connexions is something for whose existence no reason can be given. The whole pattern is arbitrarily chosen, but our feeling that we must avoid the arbitrary at this level turns out to be just another example of the vertigo referred to in chapter 3. It is possible to have the necessary connexions that are required for explanation of particular events, even though the existence of the whole scheme cannot be explained in the same way. For we see just this phenomenon in the case of language. Given that the language is as it is, the truth of one utterance can imply the truth of another, and we can explain the truth of the second by appeal to the truth of the first. But we cannot in the same way explain the existence and nature of the language itself; this remains stubbornly arbitrary.

This position may then generate the account of scientific explanation we are looking for. Instead of conceiving of natural events as isolated atomistic occurrences, related to each other only in patterns of regularities, we think of them essentially as members of a series. Indeed the individual events could not occur except as part of that series, any more than a single utterance could occur unsupported by the linguistic system of which it is a part. And the members of the series are interconnected in such a way that the other members provide a reason why this one should occur. For they stand as conditions for the truth of this one, just as it stands as a condition for their truth; this is so because each event is conceived as a *statement* to the effect that such and such other events will occur or have occurred. This being so, we have the resources required for the explanation of individual events. The explanation we offer, viz. the occurrence of other events suitably related to the first, does provide us with reasons why this one *should* have occurred, so that as the explanation grows in strength we begin to find ourselves in a situation where we can no longer conceive but that this event should have occurred. At this point our explanation is as good as explanations can be.

There are three further advantages that I want to claim for Berkeley's account of science as the attempt to learn the language of God. The first is that it enables Berkeley to say that a successful science will be the truth, and so avoid the charge that on his view any theory that succeeds in its predictions is as good as any other. For if science is the attempt to interpret the language of God, there will be as much one right answer to the questions of science as there is about what God's utterances mean. Berkeley would hold that God's meanings are simple matters of fact about which there can be right and wrong answers. The true theory will get its predictions from knowledge of these facts; other theories may predict successfully, but if they don't do it this way they will not be the truth. So Berkeley can make sense of the claim of our physics to be providing *the* truth, if physics is the interpretation of the language of God.

The second advantage is that Berkeley has a very natural answer to the question why we have a duty to seek knowledge. If we agree that the search for knowledge is intrinsically good, as well as good in its effects, we have to find some reason for saying so. Different reasons are offered. Some see this as just a special duty, that cannot be derived from or subsumed under any other.[2] For Berkeley, the attempt to understand

---

[2] Cf. J. Finnis *Fundamentals of Ethics* (Oxford: Clarendon Press 1983), pp. 50–1.

better the utterances of God has an obvious moral worth, since it is just the attempt to get closer to God. This is why he urges:

And it is the searching after, and endeavouring to understand those signs instituted by the author of nature, that ought to be the employment of the natural philosopher, and not the pretending to explain things by corporeal causes; which doctrine seems to have too much estranged the minds of men from that active principle, that supreme and wise spirit, *in whom we live, move, and have our being.* (P. 66)

The final advantage is that Berkeley can hold that a reliance on regularities in experience (such as that between clouds and rain) makes better sense if we conceive of those regularities as expressions of God's benevolence. If there is a problem about induction, or about making sense of the idea that our experience gives us reasons for beliefs about events that lie beyond our experience, Berkeley's view would be that this problem (normally known as the problem of induction) dissolves once we accept his idea of our experience as linguistic experience.

Why is it reasonable to rely on our experience? The problem of induction is that the only obvious argument that experience is reliable is that it has always proved so in the past: an argument that seems to beg the question by using experience to support experience.[3] It is as if we were to ask what reason we have to trust our prime minister and are told that our prime minister has told us that we can trust her. Berkeley's account of experience as linguistic experience offers us a way out of this conundrum. The first point is that only with experience can we even understand the natural events we encounter. Experience is necessary for the learning of any language, and this one is no exception. But, second, once we have come to understand a natural event, there is no further difficulty about our justification for believing that the world will be the way that event said it would be, i.e. for expecting certain events in the future. That justification derives from the fact that God is not a liar.

But haven't we learnt from experience that God is not a liar? Isn't our knowledge of God's benevolence derived from the useful regularity of _past_ experience? Maybe, but the point is that our hopeful beliefs about the future are as much hypotheses about the past now, since they amount to increasingly well confirmed attempts to understand the meaning of events that have already happened. It isn't that we know the nature of the past perfectly well, but are still in the dark about the future. A perfect

---

[3] The problem of induction was discovered by Hume; see his *A Treatise of Human Nature*, edited by L.A. Selby-Bigge and revised by P. Nidditch (Oxford: Clarendon Press 1978), bk. 1, pt. 3, sec. 6.

understanding of the past would itself amount to knowledge of the future.

Knowledge of a language is like knowledge of a series. If you turn out to be making mistakes about the later members of the series, or about later utterances, this in itself casts doubt on your understanding of the earlier ones. But the fact that your understanding of the earlier ones has so far proved sufficient is itself evidence that the remainder of the series will in fact go the way you think it should. Equally, there is already *some* evidence that your understanding so far is on the right lines, since it has so far proved adequate. And this means that there is already some evidence in favour of the predictions about the future that emerge from your understanding of past events.

This amounts to saying that any methodological problems there may be about translation are not related to the problem of induction. Berkeley sees the enterprise of trying to understand a natural event as analogous to that of trying to understand someone talking a foreign language, analogous, that is, to the attempt to translate. There are difficulties about translation, in particular about the idea that we can ever come to have a perfect understanding of someone else, or come to know exactly what they mean by what they say.[4] The methodology of translation is disputed, and doubts about it are real enough; but they are distinct from inductive doubts, doubts about whether our experience can give us any reason for beliefs about events beyond our experience. This means that since for Berkeley the enterprise of induction is simply one form of the attempt to translate, it cannot suffer from inductive doubts. Induction ceases to be a problem.

It seems to me then that this extension of Berkeley's position is very promising. I cannot reasonably claim that he did in fact see things in the detailed way I have argued; the few remarks on this topic in the *Principles* and in *Alciphron* are at most suggestive and not fully worked out. But I can claim that the extension is not only well within his reach but an inevitable consequence of what he does say; and that a sense of its availability may explain why Berkeley felt that his account of the natural world as the utterances of God generates a distinctive, rich and satisfying account of scientific explanation and scientific knowledge.

The world as text

It might be held that the suggestion that natural events have non-natural

---

[4] See W. V. Quine *Word and Object* (Cambridge, Mass.: MIT Press 1960), ch. 2.

meaning is anachronistic, and that it is for this reason that it cannot be attributed to Berkeley or even offered as an improvement in Berkeleian spirit. But this would be a definite mistake. Michel Foucault's studies have helped us to see that Berkeley was writing within a tradition that would find no difficulty with the thought that natural objects and events have the sort of meaning that linguistic utterances do, that the world constitutes a *text* which needs to be read (see also the early chapters of C. Taylor's *Hegel*).[5] It is a modern position to hold that the natural world is semantically inert, and not one that we can assume that Berkeley would be taking initially for granted.

There is a problem here. According to the tradition of which we are speaking, which Foucault calls the 'Renaissance Episteme', the world has the same sort of meaning as a text has, but this meaning is not an extraneous addition, due to the activity of some instilling mind. Rather it is an intrinsic feature of the world or text, and in this sense non-natural meaning emerges as a feature of the natural world. That world includes meanings rather than has them imposed on it from outside. This reveals what may by now be clear anyway, that Grice's terms 'natural' and 'non-natural' prejudicially involve an outlook which is ours, not that of the Renaissance Episteme; calling linguistic meaning non-natural just amounts to the sort of separation of linguistic meaning from the world which was one of the crucial elements of the shift from Renaissance to Classical Episteme, as Foucault saw it.

The Classical Episteme, which became prevalent with the rise of Enlightenment science, saw natural events as intrinsically devoid of semantic properties. Some events, such as the noises and the gestures we make, do have semantic properties, but those properties are added to them by an act of the mind, and the events concerned could exist without them. The Renaissance Episteme, by contrast, saw all events as significant in whatever way linguistic utterances are significant, and held that the semantic properties of the events are properties without which those events could not have existed at all. The semantic properties are intrinsic to the events, and essential to them.

If one could judge simply by the date at which he was writing, Berkeley should count as an adherent of the Classical Episteme. And this would mean that his conception of the world as text was the one available within that Episteme, namely that the significance of the events in the world is an extraneous addition to the world, caused by the operation of some

---

[5] See M. Foucault *Les Mots et Les Choses: Une Archeologie des Sciences Humaines* (Paris: Gallimard 1966), translated by A. Sheridan-Smith as *The Order of Things: An Archaeology of the Human Sciences* (New York: Random House 1970); and C. Taylor *Hegel* (Cambridge: Cambridge University Press 1975), pt. 1.

mind, and without which the world could perfectly well carry on much as before. But this seems to distort a deep element of Berkeley's position. Surely for him the natural events could not exist without their linguistic significance (their non-natural properties). The world for Berkeley is intrinsically semantic. And this means that Berkeley has to be viewed as urging the continued viability of the Renaissance Episteme, and indeed that the Classical Episteme renders incomprehensible the very science (Enlightenment science) which gave it its impetus. For Berkeley the successes of Enlightenment science are important. They persuade him that the achievements of science are the highest peak of human knowledge. But he wants to marry that science with a Renaissance view of the comprehensibility of the world.

The conception of the world as text has been a topic of lively interest in our own time, and Berkeley's version of it is worth contrasting with modern ones. As a marker, let us start by recognising a general agreement that anything that can be understood must be a text or at least like a text. This is just what Berkeley was arguing about the natural world. We can express the point by saying that to be comprehensible an object must be 'discursive' or language-like; it must in fact be what is called a 'discourse'. Given this, there are three recognisable positions about the relation between world and discourse. The first is the structuralist view that though knowledge is necessarily discursive, the world is essentially non-discursive; and hence the world itself cannot be known. The world lies beyond anything that we can reach, for the only things that we can reach are discourses, which are alien to the world. There are traces of this Kantian view in Foucault himself, though he vigorously denies that he can be called a structuralist. Anyone who holds a view of this sort is clearly influenced by the Classical Episteme, for he holds that significance is not essential to the world, and indeed that the world is essentially non-significant. This Kantian view is in marked contrast to Berkeley, and in my judgement inferior. Berkeley would say that we know perfectly well that it is false. An alternative position is that there is no world, but only discourse. This view seems rather like a form of idealism which attempts to deny the existence of material objects, rather than admit their existence while giving an idealist account of their nature. Again, Berkeley's view that there is indeed a world, and it is discursive, seems preferable.

A third strand in contemporary thought is that the world is a mass of conflicting discourses. This interesting view is associated with Foucault, a link which he would more willingly accept. But in his hands it derives from a change in the notion of a discourse. For him a discourse is any body of organised statements or *practices*; in fact he talks most freely about discursive practice, using the notion of a practice broadly. On this third view, the world is constituted by a set of discursive practices which are mutually inconsistent. Viewing it as an active text, we would have to say that it is 'polysemic', i.e. that it contains multiple and inconsistent meanings. Viewing the world as a discourse, we should say more simply that it is multiple and inconsistent. This shares an important element of Berkeley's position, since it identifies the world with discourse. But it offers a distinct contrast with Berkeley's view, which he shares with the realists, that whatever reality is it must at the least be consistent. Berkeley would argue that the world is comprehensible, and that its very comprehensibility gives us evidence that the practices that constitute it are not mutually inconsistent or polysemic. Foucault's reply would be to question the assumption that comprehensibility is necessarily evidence of consistency.

Finally, we may consider one objection to Berkeley's conception of the world as text. It seems to have left behind the idea that natural events are warnings from God about the future, instead of building on that idea as one might have expected. This is because ordinarily warnings are used to advise us of forthcoming events, in particular the unpleasant ones. But on the account I have offered it might seem that all a warning can do is to advise us of a forthcoming utterance, for all events are now conceived of as utterances. But if events are only utterances it is not clear why I should need to watch out for nasty ones; sticks and stones may break my bones but words can never hurt me, as the rhyme appositely has it.

A possible response to this objection is to accuse it of forgetting that every utterance has natural properties, in virtue of which it has its semantic ones. There could not be an event which was *only* an utterance and which had no physical properties at all; the semantic properties need the natural ones as bearers. This means that there are no purely non-natural events, in the terms we have been using. But for Berkeley there are no purely natural events either. All events have the same sort of mixture of semantic and non-semantic or natural and non-natural properties. And this means that the events we are warned about have quite sufficient nature to be genuinely unpleasant and well worth avoiding. Warnings make as much sense on this account as on any other.

I think however that this response gives the game away, by admitting too great a distinction between semantic and non-semantic properties. We argued that for Berkeley, as an adherent of the Renaissance Episteme, the events in the world could not exist without their semantic properties. But the question is why not. One can easily see why no event could have only semantic properties; the event seems after all to need a nature of some kind. But why shouldn't an event have only natural properties? The answer to this question must be that every property is both semantic and non-semantic, both natural and non-natural. This is because the nature of the property just *is* its meaning, when properly understood. Warnings do therefore make the sort of sense that they ought to; the events of which we are warned do have natural properties about 'which a warning may be welcome, but those properties are themselves significant.

In this chapter so far we have followed Berkeley's attempts to work out a conception of the natural world as a series of utterances by God. We held that his account of scientific explanation needed some supplement or other, because otherwise it was unclear how his appeal to regularities could provide anything like an explanation. Of course Berkeley could have taken other ways out of his difficulties. One such way would have been to provide a richer account of the sorts of regularities that scientific laws express, one which enables us to see how appeal to them would provide the sort of understanding of a natural event we are looking for. This way out would be more attractive to an ordinary empiricist who doesn't really want to make any essential appeal to God in order to make sense of science. And it is the way taken by Berkeley himself in some later work, particularly the *De Motu* and the *Siris*. By then, as we shall see in the next chapter, he is using the account of natural events as the language of God for another purpose: the proof of the existence of God, rather than the account of science and scientific explanation.

The benevolence of God

At the beginning of chapter 7 we considered the virtues of mechanistic explanation, and since then we have been investigating the merits of Berkeley's alternative account of scientific explanation, which we could call an interpretative or semantic account. The latter sees the regularities of the experienced world as indicative of God's benevolence; if God had not benevolently made that world comprehensible to us (interpretable, that is, or readable), we would be unable to predict the future and so act as to preserve ourselves and improve our lot. The existence of a benevolent God is a necessary condition for the success of the inter-pretative account.

There is however another sort of explanation in which the benevolence of God might play an important role, and for which Berkeley may be striving. This is the sort of explanation sometimes called teleological. Properly, teleological explanation should be explanation in terms of someone's purposes, so that a teleological explanation of the course of nature would amount to showing how that course served to further those purposes. In Berkeley's case, those purposes would of course be God's purposes.

Teleological explanation in this sense might seem to be incompatible with the interpretative explanations we have been talking about, since explanations in terms of purposes seem to impute a direction to the world they explain. The world is travelling a certain path because God intends that it should travel that path, because of where it will end up if it does. Interpretative explanations, on the other hand, though they do provide us with the material needed to make successful predictions about the future, are strictly symmetrical between past and future. Each event on that account is as much a statement about the past as it is about the future.

This way of seeing things would leave teleological explanations incompatible with interpretative ones. But there is a broader sense of purpose, in which the fact that the world is serving God's purposes does not imply that it is going in any direction. It would be sufficient for this sense of purpose, for instance, that God should intend the world to be generally as pleasant as possible for us. Such an intention is not really a matter of a direction in which the world is travelling. It is symmetrical between past and future in just the sort of way that interpretative explanation requires. And Berkeley does think that God has such an intention. The question is why he thinks this, and what sort of role it plays in his account of our ability to understand the world.

The important thing to notice is that the sort of benevolence at issue in the thought that God wishes the world to be as pleasant for us as possible seems much greater than the sort required merely to explain the consistency of experience. If God's benevolence is revealed merely by the consistency of the experienced world, it seems a rather thin sort of benevolence. After all, the world could surely be consistent and hence predictable, but consistently nasty rather than consistently pleasant. If it were consistently nasty, it would hardly be the creation of a fully benevolent God. God's benevolence, then, if it plays a role in teleological explanations of the natural world, must play a double role. The first part is provided by the account of explanation as interpretation, hinging only on the requirement that a benevolent God be consistent. The second part is provided by the idea that God wants our world to be consistently pleasant.

Someone who thinks that God is benevolent in the stronger sense will want to use this fact in generating explanations, not of particular events, but of the general course of nature, and perhaps also of the fact that there is a world of sense at all. Such explanations are vulnerable to the charge that the world is unnecessarily unpleasant. This charge is sometimes referred to as the problem of pain. Surely if God were really benevolent there would be no such thing as pain. This complaint is easily dismissed by showing that pain is a useful indicator of possible damage. Without pain life would be more dangerous and unpleasant rather than less so. But the complaint recurs, in the charge that even so there is a quite unnecessary amount of pain and suffering. Berkeley replies to this charge in passages towards the end of the *Principles*, where he argues that our belief that any pain or suffering is unnecessary derives entirely from ignorance. He writes:

As for the mixture of pain or uneasiness which is in the world, pursuant to the general laws of Nature, and the actions of finite imperfect spirits: this, in the state we are in at present, is indispensably necessary to our well-being. But our prospects are too narrow: we take, for instance, the idea of some one particular pain into our thoughts, and account it *evil*; whereas if we enlarge our view, so as to comprehend the various ends, connexions, and dependencies of things, on what occasions and in what proportions we are affected with pain and pleasure, the nature of human freedom, and the design with which we are put into the world; we shall be forced to acknowledge that those particular things, which considered in themselves appear to be *evil*, have the nature of *good*, when considered as linked with the whole system of beings. (P. 153)

Berkeley, then, takes it that the world God provides is the best possible. And if this were so, explanations of the course of nature could appeal not only to the consistency of that course, but also to its consistent goodness. It is not just that things do go this way, but also that it is best that they should. The question for Berkeley is whether he knows that the world we live in is the best possible because he knows that God is benevolent, or whether he knows that God is benevolent because he knows that the world is the best possible. It seems evident that it must be the first of these. But in that case Berkeley needs some evidence for the benevolence of God over and above that which shows that God is benevolent by appealing to the consistency of the world. For, as we said, it seems quite possible that the world should be consistently nasty. How does Berkeley know that God's goodness is greater than that required to explain the consistency of the world?

It seems from the text that Berkeley simply inferred God's benevolence from the consistency. For instance, he writes:

And yet this consistent uniform working, which so evidently displays the goodness and wisdom of that governing spirit . . . (P. 32)

and:

we shall, from the constant uniform method of our sensations, collect the goodness and wisdom of the *spirit* who excites them in our minds. (P. 72)

This does make it appear that Berkeley's view of God as benevolent derives entirely and mistakenly from his thought that the ideas of sense are consistent. What seems to be needed is a passage where Berkeley argues directly that God is benevolent, over and above being wise, consistent and powerful. But I do not know of any such. Does this discover a lacuna in Berkeley's philosophy? I think that Berkeley would argue that an orderly but evil world is inconsistent. We have been taking it to be obvious that the world could be consistently unpleasant, but Berkeley would say that if there is an evil spirit, his operations would not be readable by us because he would take care that they were not. The mere fact that the world of sense is comprehensible is evidence, then, that God is benevolent in the stronger sense. The intermediate hypothesis that the world might be consistently nasty is only consistent with an evil God who is incompetent or who does not know his own mind. But the consistency of the world of sense is itself evidence that the powerful spirit who creates the ideas of sense is extremely competent and does indeed know his own mind. So the intermediate hypothesis is ruled out, and the consistency of the world of sense does establish directly the benevolence of God.

This generates the traditional result that an evil world is incomprehensible. For such a world would be one which did not contain sufficient orderliness to support scientific explanation. Whether explanation is thought of as mechanical or interpretative, it requires regularity; so since evil would make regularity impossible, an evil world could not be explained.

How do teleological explanations of this type fit with interpretative explanations? Are we really clear that they do not compete? As long as we held, against Berkeley, that there were different degrees of benevolence required for the different styles of explanation, it was easy to see room for saying that the two sorts of explanation are different, and even that they answer different questions. We suggested that interpretative explanations address themselves to questions about particular events, while teleological explanations answer questions about the general course of nature, and about the very existence of a world of sense. But this now seems dubious, for with the collapse of the distinction between the benevolence required for consistency and that required to make the world the best possible, what can teleological explanations add to what interpretative ones have already provided? The crucial question is whether a perfect interpretative understanding of the world would itself constitute recognition that this world is the best possible. If it would not, what more would be required?

One might think that there are here two routes to the knowledge that this world is the best possible. The first we have already seen; if the very comprehensibility of the world establishes the benevolence of God (in the strong sense), it also serves to establish that God could not have created a better world than this. The second route is via the future success of science. We begin to take this route when we begin to comprehend "the various ends, connexions, and dependencies of things" (from P. 153, quoted above). For Berkeley, science should eventually lead to a perfect interpretative understanding. With that understanding, we will no doubt be lost in admiration for the "divine traces of wisdom and goodness that shine through the economy of Nature" (P. 154). But I see no reason to suppose that this itself will be enough for us to recognise that no better system could be found, if we did not already have sufficient reason to believe so. We will, in a sense, see the reason for everything; for each event, we will know why it is so. But our knowledge will still be internal, for understanding an event will be the same as seeing how it fits into the scheme of things. We need further reason to suppose that there could not be a better scheme, which knowledge of the scheme will not itself provide.

It seems, then, that teleological explanations are supplementary to interpretative ones. In my view, Berkeley thinks of himself as offering both. Our final question is whether the resulting position is preferable to that of a religious mechanist. At the beginning of chapter 7 I mentioned that Berkeley is more diffident about his philosophy of science, holding only that he can give as rich an account of scientific explanation as that of his realist rival. We have already seen that this modesty is misplaced, but it may be that Berkeley's system enjoys one final advantage, derived from the fact that God gets into his story earlier, at the level of the explanation of particular events.

Berkeley does of course have criticisms of the mechanistic account. He says that we cannot conceive of material objects acting as causes in the way that it requires, and that mechanism, in thinking of those objects as intermediary causes, diminishes the glory of God in imputing to him either the need to use intermediaries or the adoption of an unnecessary and therefore inexplicable manner of operation. It is surely the latter point which we can use for our present purposes. The general thrust will be that the subsequent addition of a benevolent God to a basically mechanistic system creates a whole which is centrally incoherent, since the second part removes the need for the first. The enormous machine which is the mechanists' world turns out in the end to be explanatorily redundant. Berkeley's own account has no such redundant elements, and a scheme without redundancy of this sort is a better, because tighter, explanation.

In summary, then, this chapter has tried to show a richness and unity in Berkeley's account of scientific knowledge and scientific explanation, and in particular that our sense of a necessary connexion between distinct events can be restored by interpretative or semantic explanations; and that teleological explanations of the course of nature can be added to interpretative explanations to provide a satisfying whole.

9

Spirits

As we have seen in earlier chapters, scepticism comes in varying forms or degrees. We have considered two such forms: scepticism about the possibility of knowledge and scepticism about understanding; and our general view has been that both are interesting, but that Berkeley is more concerned with sceptical arguments of the first sort than with those of the second. It is, however, more common nowadays to discern three forms of scepticism rather than just two. The first of these is about the possibility of knowledge, as before, and this is held to be the least interesting of the three. But it would be possible to admit that we can never get knowledge in some area while still insisting that some of our beliefs in that area are better supported and more probably true than others, and therefore that it is possible for our beliefs there to be *justified*, at least, even if they can never be *knowledge*. The second form of scepticism denies even this. Not only cannot we know any proposition to be true, but we cannot have sufficient reason or even any reason to believe one thing rather than another. This position may appear extreme and counter-intuitive, but the philosophical tradition contains several strong arguments for it. The Pyrrhonists held that the reasons in favour of a belief are never any better than the reasons against; Hume argued that there can be no such thing as one belief counting as a reason in favour of another. But of course we might have less general reasons than these for holding that beliefs of a certain restricted sort can never be justified: beliefs, say, about the remote future or about God. And in such a case our scepticism would be local rather than global; some beliefs would escape its net.

But it is the third and strongest sort of scepticism which will matter most for our purposes in this chapter. This scepticism claims that we cannot even understand the propositions which the previous scepticism said we could never be justified in believing. Now a scepticism of this third sort is not likely to be completely general or global; no sceptic is likely to claim that we don't understand any proposition whatever, if only because this would leave the sceptical claim itself apparently beyond our understanding. But the second and third scepticisms might differ in less general claims. For instance, the second might hold that though we understand propositions about God well enough we never have sufficient evidence to justify believing that any of them are true. The third would hold that propositions about God are incomprehensible. We can't understand them, and *a fortiori* could never be justified in believing them true; to do so would be to contend for something without knowing what.

I said that the first form of scepticism, that which is about the possibility of knowledge, is held to be the less interesting than is scepticism about the possibility of justified belief. This fact reveals a change in the climate of opinion from Berkeley's time, and results from a change in background assumptions. In chapter 6 I discussed a Berkeleian assumption to the effect that human knowledge is to be conceived on the model of God's knowledge, and the effects that this had on contemporary sceptical arguments. One of the effects of Berkeley's assumption here is to render scepticism about knowledge at least as interesting as that about justified belief. Without that assumption, however, it is possible to accept the loss of knowledge without too much chagrin, provided that one is able to retain justified belief. Maybe I never really *know* that there are real physical objects around me, but at least I have very good reasons to believe that there are some. Much contemporary philosophy has gone into showing how this thought might come out true, tacitly or explicitly admitting that the possibility of knowledge is not worth the struggle required to save it. Berkeley's position would, I think, have been that once one has admitted that knowledge is impossible there is nothing much left worth fighting for.

The importance of these distinctions will emerge in this chapter; we have already seen something of it in chapter 2. There we saw that Berkeley does wield against Locke a sceptical argument which is of our first two sorts. I say of our first two sorts, because although it looked like one of the first sort because it is overtly concerned with our lack of knowledge of the realist's material world, it also argues that realism cannot mention a single reason for believing that there is such a world. Berkeley writes:

But though it were possible that solid, figured, moveable substances may exist without the mind, . . . yet how is it possible for us to know this? Either we must know it by sense, or by reason. As for our senses, . . . they do not inform us that things exist without the mind, or unperceived, like to those which are perceived . . . It remains therefore that . . . it must be by reason, inferring their existence from what is immediately perceived by sense. But what reason can induce us to believe the existence of bodies without the mind, from what we perceive, since . . . it is possible that we might be affected with all the ideas we have now, though no bodies existed without, resembling them. (P. 18)

I have commented before on this argument and its many defects. The defects do not matter, however, because Berkeley's main argument against Locke is not a scepticism of the first two sorts, but of the third sort. He writes:

What you contend for, is a downright contradiction. . . . I am content to put the whole upon this issue; if you can but conceive it possible for one extended moveable substance . . . to exist otherwise than in a mind perceiving it . . . I shall . . . grant you its existence, though you cannot either give me any reason why you believe it exists, or assign any use to it when it is supposed to exist. I say, the bare possibility of your opinion's being true, shall pass for an argument that it is so. (P. 22)

Berkeley then takes the strongest possible line against Locke's realism about material objects. But Locke held that there are two sorts of things or substances, material substances and immaterial substances. The latter are the minds or spirits about whose existence Berkeley has no qualms; the former are the things which he held to be incomprehensible. The question with which this chapter is concerned is whether this position is consistent, or whether Berkeley's arguments against material substance are not equally effective against immaterial substance, mind or spirit. For us this amounts to the question whether the argument against abstraction abolishes the immaterial substances along with the material ones, which would reduce Berkeley's idealism to absurdity. Berkeleian ideas are dependent entities and cannot exist by themselves; they need spirits to exist in. Remove the spirits and there is nothing independent in the world, just ideas searching in vain for something to belong to.

Berkeley needs to provide us with a two-fold account of minds or spirits, an account which answers two questions. First we need to know how we come to understand talk about spirits, and second we need to be told what sorts of evidence we have that there are any such things. Of course, it may be that the answer to the first question also generates an answer to the second. Wherever we want to say that we understand talk about a certain sort of thing by coming across examples of things of that sort, we have no need to look further for an answer to the second question. And Berkeley's answer to the first question is indeed that we come to understand talk about spirits by coming across one of them, namely ourselves. He expresses himself most clearly on these matters in the Third Dialogue (pp. 232–4):

My own mind and my own ideas I have an immediate knowledge of; and by the help of these, do mediately apprehend the possibility of the existence of other spirits and ideas.

and

The being of myself, that is, my own soul, mind or thinking principle, I evidently know by reflection.

and

How often must I repeat, that I know or am conscious of my own being; and that I myself am not my ideas, but somewhat else, a thinking active principle that perceives, knows, wills, and operates about ideas.

But in the case of spirits there is an added complication. Our knowledge of ourselves seems on this Berkeleian account to be a special sort of knowledge. However we are to understand it exactly, we know of our own existence in a way in which we could not come to know of the existence of others. In which case, though we already know how we know there to be *one* spirit, we still need to know what sort of evidence we have that there are others, and even before that we need to know how it is that there *can* be any others like that one. For it may be that the peculiar way we have of finding out our own existence makes it difficult for us to conceive of there being other beings like ourself. This is the traditional problem of Other Minds, which is so thorny that it is normally dignified by capital letters.

So how does Berkeley handle this problem? He seems to see no difficulty in the direct claim that once we have established the existence of one spirit we have thereby established the possibility of more than one:

My own mind and my own ideas I have an immediate knowledge of; and by the help of these, do mediately apprehend the *possibility* of the existence of other spirits. [as above, with my stress]

This claim is dubious, as we shall see. But given that we do know that there *might* be other minds than our own, what evidence do we have that there actually are any such? The answer is:

From what hath been said, it is plain that we cannot know the existence of other spirits, otherwise than by their operations, or the ideas by them excited in us. I perceive several motions, changes, and combinations of ideas, that inform me there are certain particular agents like myself, which accompany them, and concur in their production. Hence the knowledge I have of other spirits is not immediate, as is the knowledge of my ideas; but depending on the intervention of ideas, by me referred to agents or spirits distinct from myself, as effects or concomitant signs. (P. 145) and:

Moreover, as we conceive the ideas that are in the minds of other spirits by means of our own, which we suppose to be resemblances of them: so we know other spirits by means of our own soul, which in that sense is the image or idea of them, it having a like respect to other spirits, that blueness or heat by me perceived hath to those ideas perceived by another. (P. 140)

So the possibility of other minds is easily procured, for they are just further beings like ourselves, and their actual existence we know by the ideas they cause in us. Presumably Berkeley has in mind here things like the statements they make and the machines they create. The ideas that others cause *are* the statements and the machines, not the ideas we have in response to them. But we shall have to wait till later to see whether this is right.

The mind as an active principle

We need now to examine more closely the way in which this system is supposed to work. How does Berkeley conceive of the object whose existence we know immediately, and what sort of knowledge is this immediate knowledge? Early in the Principles, he writes:

A spirit is one simple, undivided, active being: as it perceives ideas, it is called the *understanding*, and as it produces or otherwise operates about them, it is called the *will*. (P. 27)

What does Berkeley mean by calling spirits active beings? As we have seen in chapter 4, he insists that ideas are passive and only spirits active. At *Principles* 139 he says that a spirit is "that which perceives ideas, and wills, and reasons about them". Is a spirit active in all these respects, or only in some? Berkeley seems to think of us as passive in perception, since in perception we are receiving ideas from without, and active in imagination. But leaving perception non-active in this way has its problems. It is in danger of breaking the mind up into separate and dissimilar parts, with consequent difficulties in the idea that we can somehow be aware of the whole thing at once. This will be especially true if we hold that it is through its status as an active principle that our mind is known to us. How would such a method reveal to us the non-active side of the mind? Berkeley does seem to court this danger at *Principles* 28, where he cites only the operations of the imagination to show that the mind is active:

I find I can excite ideas in my mind at pleasure, and vary and shift the scene as oft as I think fit. It is no more than willing, and straightway this or that idea arises in my fancy ... This making and unmaking of ideas doth very properly denominate the mind active.

But that danger is not the only one for him here. He also faces the question how to make sense of what we more normally think of as human agency, in particular the ability to move our bodies at will. Berkeley wants to give a sense to the idea that we can do this and need not rely on God to do it for us by agreeing to make available the relevant ideas of sense. This emerges in the Third Dialogue, where he is trying to argue that our actions are the effects of our wills so that we rather than God should get the blame (and credit) for them:

It is true, I have denied there are any other agents besides spirits: but this is very consistent with allowing to thinking rational beings, in the production of motions, the use of limited powers, ultimately indeed derived from God, but immediately under the direction of their own wills, which is sufficient to entitle them to all the guilt of their actions. (p. 237)

But in suggesting that it is in the imagination that we are primarily active Berkeley shows that he is thinking of action or activity in a way that is going to make it hard for him to think of the apparently more normal case of agency, our moving our own bodies about, as activity in the same sense. So in stressing our nature as active principles Berkeley faces several problems. First, do we have some non-active part (e.g. in perception) and if so how does it fit in with the active part? How can we be a principle which is active but not purely active? Second, how can we give an uniform account of agency, of what it is to be an agent, which fits both our ability to conjure up ideas of the imagination at will and our ability to act, i.e. to move our bodies at will (if this is what acting in this sense is)?

Perhaps the answer to the first question is that we are partially active even in perception. There are two passages that allow us to think that this may be Berkeley's view:

But whatever power I may have over my own thoughts, I find the ideas actually perceived by sense have not a like dependence on my will. (P. 29)

The ideas of sense are ... less dependent on the spirit, or thinking substance which perceives them, in that they are excited by the will of another and more powerful spirit. (P. 33)

Notice the phrase "not a like dependence"; Berkeley may only be admitting here that the ideas of sense are not dependent on my will in the way that the ideas of the imagination are. Perhaps they are dependent on it in some other way. And the second remark suggests that these two ways are not so different as to be unable to be compared with one another. The ideas of sense are less dependent on the will than are the ideas of the imagination. So it seems that we have not here two distinct notions of dependence, as one might at first suspect. What then does Berkeley have in mind when he suggests that the ideas of sense are to some extent dependent on the will of the spirit that perceives them? Among the possibilities are that though we don't choose what we see, we can and do affect what we see by choosing where to look, and can prevent an idea of sense by keeping our eyes tight shut. Another more subtle idea would be that we contribute to the order in which the ideas of sense are arrayed; the order of scanning is the order of presentation, and this is something which is not determined for us by the ideas of sense themselves. We are forced to resort here to more arcane sources of evidence, since the *Principles* and *Dialogues* offer no help. But in his notebooks, otherwise known as the *Philosophical Commentaries*, Berkeley makes several relevant remarks. Entry 821 reads "Understanding is in some sort an action" and entry 833 contains a curious argument:

It seems there can be no perception, no idea without will, being there are no ideas so indifferent but one had rather have them than annihilation, or annihilation than them. or if there be such an equal balance there must be an equal mixture of pleasure & pain to cause it. there being no ideas perfectly void of all pain & uneasiness but what are preferable to annihilation.

This seems to be an attempt to argue that every idea, whether of sense or not, is an object of the will since every idea is attended by pleasure, pain or at least uneasiness. Hence our acceptance or reception of any idea is a form of acquiescence. (Berkeley is not arguing that every idea is preferable to death and the annihilation of the self.) The point is that either having an idea is preferable to not having it or *vice versa*, but either way the occurrence of the idea is a matter for the will. The will may not always be effective in such matters, particularly in the avoidance of pain, but it is at least involved. And Berkeley never contracted to argue that we have the same control over the ideas of sense as we have over those of the imagination; we have the same sort of control, but a lesser degree of it. We might object that he has muddled two points here, one about control and one about our minds not being indifferent to the ideas they are fed. It might be accepted that perception is not just the blank passing of ideas, since there is to be considered also our response to them. But this does nothing to show that we have any degree of control over the ideas of sense.

Further discussion of this topic seems unprofitable, and we can perhaps leave it for our second question about Berkeley's conception of the mind.

Human agency

Is the sort of agency involved in acts of the imagination to be conceived as identical with the sort of agency involved in human bodily movement? So far we have decided that the spirit is somehow uniformly active. But we are going to have to face the question how we come to know the existence of this active principle, and our answer will be affected by the question what sort of agency is at issue. Is it in the acts of the imagination that we peculiarly reveal ourselves to ourselves, or is it in moving about the world, or both?

The question is not, or at least not yet, whether Berkeley can make good sense of the notion of human agency as normally conceived. Rather we have to try to say what it is about the imagination that reveals us to us, and whether the same feature is present in acting. For if not, again the entity revealed to us is not, or not yet, the entity that moves around the world at will, and we only 'know ourselves as an active principle' in a rather incomplete sense.

Now the reason why it is hard to see imagination and action as agency in the same sense is that in the case of the imagination our will seems to be in complete control in a way that it is not in complete control of the body. Normally, at least, we do not rely on the existence of suitable external conditions in order to be able to imagine the things we decide to imagine. But with bodily movement the matter is different, as is shown by a famous experiment of William James', the American philosopher and psychologist.[1] The subject of this experiment was anaesthetised in the arm and then blindfolded; and then his arm was strapped to his body so that he could not move it. He was then told to raise his arm. Nothing happened, of course; or at least the arm did not go up. But the subject himself thought that he had raised his arm. To him it seemed that he had done everything normally required for his arm to go up. Whatever it is that willing is, he did it this time. And of course if there is such a thing as the will this is true, but it only shows that our will relies here on something which it is not itself able to provide. And this distinguishes bodily action from the activity of the imagination. They do not seem both to be action in the same sense.

[1] See W. James *The Principles of Psychology* (New York: Dover 1950), II, 105.

One conclusion we might draw from this is that bodily action is not really action proper at all. True action cannot depend in this way on the existence of suitable external conditions. Bodily movement is not therefore an activity of the *will*, but rather a normal effect of certain activities of the will. We will, and then if we are lucky bits of our bodies move in the way we meant them to. To take this line would indeed resolve Berkeley's problems for him here. But it has obvious defects, most clearly seen in the views of one of Berkeley's contemporaries, namely the Occasionalism to be found in Malebranche's *De La Recherche De La Verité*.

Malebranche held that bodily movement occurs when God connives with the 'choices' which we make. We choose to raise an arm, and God takes that choice as the occasion for him to make our arm go up. This theory succeeds in showing that, and how, things generally happen to our bodies the way we want them to. But it has two defects, the second more important for our purposes than the first. The first is that it fails to show that we, the choosers, bear the responsibility for our actions and their consequences. It seems that at the very least God, as conniver, must bear some of that responsibility. This complaint might not matter too much; we might seem still to bear some part of the responsibility, which is perhaps all that is required to justify our getting the blame. But this is only so if we still count as agents, as the ones who do the actions. And the main weakness of Occasionalism is that it seems to make God the only agent; he is the one who really does the actions, not us. Occasionalism fails as a theory of *moral* agency because it fails as a theory of *human* agency.

Berkeley tackles the problem of moral responsibility, making Hylas say:

You are not aware, Philonous, that in making God the immediate author of all the motions in nature, you make him the author of murder, sacrilege, adultery, and the like heinous sins. (p. 236)

Philonous' reply is twofold. First he argues that he who conceives or wishes the sin bears the brunt of the blame:

Sin or moral turpitude does not consist in the outward physical action or motion, but in the internal deviation of the will from the laws of reason and religion.

Second he complains more pertinently that

I have nowhere said that God is the only agent who produces all the motions in bodies. It is true, I have denied that there are any other agents besides spirits: but this is very consistent with allowing to thinking rational beings, in the production of motions, the use of limited powers, ultimately indeed derived from God, but immediately under the direction of their own wills, which is sufficient to entitle them to all the guilt of their actions. (p. 237)

The first of these replies, if effective at all, was equally available to Malebranche. One should remember here that most theological views have at least some trouble with the notion of human moral responsibility. But normally this is because of God's omniscience; God knows what we are going to do, and so bears part of the blame because he chose not to prevent us. This of course assumes that we count as agents. Berkeley and Malebranche are in special trouble here because they seem unable to give a sense to the notion of human agency at all, shared or otherwise. So it is the second reply that is crucial. Berkeley wants to say that he can manage to give a genuine sense to the idea that there are agents other than God. And this is very hard for him within the confines of his system.

The particular problem for Berkeley is that the bodily movements that are the intended results of the operations of our will are ideas of sense, on his showing. And as such they are the creations of God, not the doings of the person who 'intended' them. In fact, at its most extreme, Berkeley's position is that every bodily movement, like every other natural event, is an utterance of God. But how much room does this leave for the claim that there are any agents other than God? There are other agents in the thin sense that we are free to imagine what we will; but there is no sense in which we are free to move around the world. Movement of this sort is the province of God, by which we do not mean that God is the only object that moves, but rather that God is the only cause of natural events such as movements. If we don't cause the movements of our bodies, how can it be true that some of those movements are actions of ours?

Berkeley could of course say that God chooses to make available to us the relevant ideas of sense when we make suitable 'choices'. I put the word 'choices' in inverted commas here because these are not choices as ordinarily conceived. But this just reveals the weakness of this reply, the weakness of Occasionalism. We aren't really agents on this account at all. Everything that we want to count as an action is done by God.

Is there any room for manoeuvre here? It is no use trying to escape by saying that we are at least partially responsible for the ideas of sense we perceive, on the grounds that we have at least to decide whether to open our eyes and in which direction to look; what we then see may indeed be up to God, but we did make this minimal contribution. This won't work because it simply begs the question. Opening our eyes and turning our heads are among the events which we are now finding it hard to see as actions of ours, on Berkeley's account. What is needed is to find a way of saying that God has handed over to us the control of certain ideas of sense, i.e. those bodily movements which are our actions. But it is not easy to see how to do this. Any move which requires God still to exercise his will on the occasion of each exercise of our wills is likely to leave us feeling that we are agents in at best a very watered-down sense. Perhaps then we have to conceive of God as having made a once and for all decision at the Creation that in suitable situations (i.e. when the 'decisions' we are making concern movements of our own bodies, and there are no special circumstances such as those of the William James experiment) the world should change in whatever ways we may will that it should. This intermediate position ascribes the sort of joint responsibility that Berkeley seems to have wanted.

In different terms, the idea here is that we can distinguish between standing and occurrent causes for a given event. For the occurrence of a fire, for instance, there must be oxygen; and there must also be some trigger such as the lighting of a match. The presence of the oxygen is necessary for the fire, and so is the lighting of the match, but they stand in different relations to the fire they combine to cause. The presence of the oxygen counts as a standing cause, a permanent situation without which nothing could trigger a fire. The lighting of the match counts as the occurrent cause, the change in circumstance which led to the fire. Berkeley could say that God's decision at the Creation to implement such acts of will as we make in suitable situations establishes a permanent situation of willingness which is the standing cause of any action we perform, while our acts of will count as occurrent causes for those actions.

This approach allows us to explain our sense that it is really we that are to blame for our actions, even though God is somehow causally implicated. This is just a further instance of our normal tendency, other things being equal, to count the occurrent cause of an event as its *real* cause. In the example of the fire, we would naturally think of the lighting of the match as the cause, and ascribe blame in that direction if anywhere.

Of course God cannot opt out completely. Berkeley would not be willing to say, as some do, that God can disclaim responsibility on the grounds of ignorance of our future intentions. He has no such ignorance, being omniscient. God decides in advance to cooperate in our enterprises, in full knowledge of what those enterprises will be. So he is implicated; he connives. But we have avoided the occasionalist view that each of our 'choices' is the occasion of an independent act of will on the part of God. This view would amount to the suggestion that for each action of ours there is a separate act of God's will as an occurrent rather than a standing cause. Malebranche held this, but Berkeley did not.

Even if we can impute this position to Berkeley, there remains a considerable difficulty. This is that if we avoid the Scylla of making God the real author and cause of all the bodily movements that we originally thought of as our own doings, we fall into the Charybdis of holding that the bodily movements of which we are the cause are not real things. This is because real things are those ideas which are more independent of the mind that perceives them, and the bodily movements, though *qua* natural events they should count as ideas of sense, are slipping back into the control of the minds that conceive them. So the more we regain a sense of control over our own actions, the less those actions will count as part of the real world. Sadly, I do not think that the distinction between standing and occurrent causes will help us out of this difficulty. But perhaps some sort of reply is available to Berkeley here. A bodily movement is an idea of sense, and as such it can be perceived by more than one mind. Since for the vast majority of those minds it counts happily as an idea that is less dependent on them, it is a real thing. And this is so even though it has the peculiar status of being more dependent than are most ideas of sense on one particular mind; so this special relation to one mind need not be taken to deprive it of reality.

This is the best I can offer on Berkeley's behalf here; one cannot deny that he has real problems in making genuine sense of our status as agents in a public world, a world in which we *move*. Let us now return to the point at which we became embroiled in these difficulties.

The nature of the self

Berkeley holds that we are directly aware of ourselves as an active principle, and indirectly aware of the existence of other minds like ourselves because of the ideas which they cause. We were asking exactly how this system is supposed to work. Using the results we have already reached, we may presume that Berkeley wants to say that some of our ideas of sense are relevantly similar to those of which we know that we have a comparative degree of control (under God's permission). These are the movements of bodies that are like ours but are not ours. Inferring from our own case, we come to the view that probably there are other minds like ourselves, each blessed with its own localised sphere of comparative control.

This then is the end of the story. What comes in the middle? The middle is our ability to conceive of the *possibility* that there be another object like ourself. This possibility depends crucially upon our conception of ourself, to which we therefore return. Why does the fact that we are active beings explain our knowledge of ourselves? Or, to put it another way, what is it about acting that gives the agent a peculiar insight into his own existence, an insight that no-one could have into the existence of another?

We can approach this question by looking at a difficulty which Berkeley himself raised in the Third Dialogue. There Hylas makes two points, both of which follow from the same premise. This is the central Berkeleian tenet that no idea can resemble anything but another idea. If this is so, no idea can resemble a mind. And this is particularly obvious when we remember that ideas are essentially passive and minds essentially active. How could a passive thing resemble an active one, or, to put it another way, how could an object of awareness bear any resemblance to awareness itself or to the will? To Berkeley it seemed clear that it could not. Already at the beginning of the Principles he wrote:

Hence there can be no idea formed of a soul or spirit: for all ideas whatever, being passive and inert, *vide* sect. 25. they cannot represent unto us, by way of image or likeness, that which acts. (P. 27)

Hylas draws two conclusions from this. First he argues that the notion of a spirit or mental substance is no more coherent than the idea of a physical object or material substance, so that Berkeley must either retain substances of both sorts in his system or abandon them both, with obviously disastrous consequences.

No idea can be like a spirit. We have therefore no idea of any spirit. You admit nevertheless that there is spiritual substance, although you have no idea of it; while you deny there can be such a thing as material substance, because you have no notion or idea of it. Is this fair dealing? To act consistently, you must either admit matter or reject spirit. What say you to this? (p. 232)

Berkeley has no trouble with some of this attack. He makes two points. First, he says that his original objection to material substance was not that he had no idea of it, but that "in the very notion or definition of material substance, there is included a manifest repugnance and inconsistency". Since there is no such inconsistency in the notion of a spirit, that notion can happily be retained. Second, he has no reason for believing in the existence of matter, "whereas the being of myself, that is, my own soul, mind or thinking principle, I evidently know by reflection". So far he is on firm enough ground. But Hylas had a second point which is more damaging, and which he repeats:

Notwithstanding all you have said, to me it seems, that according to your own way of thinking, and in consequence of your own principles, it should follow that you are only a system of floating ideas, without any substance to support them. Words are not to be used without a meaning. And as there is no more meaning in spiritual substance than in material substance, the one is to be exploded as well as the other. (p. 233)

Hylas is suggesting that on Berkeley's principles to understand something is to have an idea of it, and to have an idea of something is to have an idea that resembles it. But we cannot have an idea that resembles a mind or spirit, and hence we cannot have an idea of a mind, and hence we cannot understand talk about minds; such talk is meaningless. The only sort of talk we can understand, then, is talk about ideas. And this means that we can make no sense of the suggestion that as well as our ideas there is an object, the mind or spirit, which is distinct from them and which *has* them or which *perceives* them. Our conception of ourselves, then, must be a conception of a package of ideas which is not supported by or owned by an object. We must therefore be nothing but "a system of floating ideas", floating in the sense that I am my ideas, not an object distinct from them which grounds them (to continue the metaphor of flotation).

This is a very serious charge. Berkeley wants to say that ideas cannot exist except in a mind, and that the mind they exist in is an entity distinct from them, which has them or to which they are present. But it looks as if he is not going to be able to do this. His response is to claim that though he has no idea of a mind or spirit, he still has some *notion* of such a thing, some mental grasp on what it is to be such a thing. Of course he has to explain how one could come to have such a notion; but he is adamant that this can be done:

I say lastly, that I have a notion of spirit, though I have not, strictly speaking, an idea of it. I do not perceive it as an idea, or by means of an idea, but know it by reflection . . . How often must I repeat, that I know or am conscious of my own being; and that I myself am not my ideas, but somewhat else, a thinking active principle that perceives, knows, wills, and operates about ideas. (p. 233–4: see also P. 137–40)

The question then is whether Berkeley can make good his claim that we can derive a 'notion' of a mind from our own case, i.e. by what he calls reflection. For if he cannot, he is condemned to a position in which the mind or self is conceived of only as a collection of ideas rather than as an independent existent. Hume, who was obviously greatly impressed by Berkeley's arguments here, took it that no matter how hard we concentrate on ourselves we never become aware of (even in the weakest possible sense of 'having a notion of') anything other than what Berkeley would call an idea:

For my part, when I enter most intimately into what I call *myself*, I always stumble on some particular perception or other, of heat or cold, light or shade, love or hatred, pain or pleasure. I never can catch *myself* at any time without a perception, and never can observe anything but the perception.[2]

But it is not simply a question of what happens when we try to focus on ourselves rather than on some idea of ours. Hume presents it as if it were a simple matter of fact that this procedure does not work. But Hylas' point was that on Berkeley's principles it is not a simple matter of fact. The reason why one never catches oneself without a perception, and only ever catches the perception, is that selves are not the sort of things of which there *can* be perceptions. Berkeley himself, in the person of Hylas, has shown us one way in which this result emerges. But there is another. For, as we shall now see, the argument from abstraction, which is the argument that shows the inconceivability of matter, seems also to show the inconceivability of other minds. And if other minds are inconceivable, we are going to find it hard to hold that our own mind is something of which we can get a conception; for if we could get a conception of one, surely we should be able to get a conception of another. This is a different and more complex route to the same conclusion, that we cannot conceive of ourselves any more than we can conceive of others. The mind, if it is to be something distinct from ideas which supports them by owning them, emerges as something inconceivable.

Our knowledge of other minds

Can I conceive of something as able to exist unconceived? Berkeley's negative answer to this question depended upon his assertion that it is impossible to abstract from anything we can conceive (any idea, that is) its relation to a mind, so as to conceive it or anything like it existing unconceived. Neither can we conceive of anything as able to exist out of all relation to a mind. Suppose that we accept this for present purposes. Similar arguments may be used to prove conclusions more damning to Berkeley; they will show that this style of argument proves too much, and that there must therefore be something wrong with it (without of course showing what).

There are two ways in which one might hope to come to conceive of the existence of minds other than oneself. The first is by conceiving of ideas as existing or as able to exist in another mind, and so conceiving of

[2] D. Hume *A Treatise of Human Nature*, edited by L.A. Selby-Bigge and revised by P. Nidditch (Oxford: Clarendon Press 1978), bk. 1 pt. 4 sec. 6, at p. 252.

that other mind by way of its content. The second is to conceive of the other mind directly as another owner like oneself.

The first question then is whether I can conceive of an idea as able to exist in a mind other than mine. If I can't do this, I am condemned to a very strong form of solipsism, the view that all possible experiences are mine. And it does seem that the arguments wielded in chapter 3 support this view. To conceive of an idea as able to exist in another mind and not in my own is to conceive of it as existing in relation to some mind or other but not in relation to any particular mind. But this sort of determinable but not determinate relation to a mind is just the sort of abstract conception that Berkeley elsewhere takes such exception to. He will not allow that we can conceive of an object as having some colour or other but no particular colour; and equally he should not allow that we can conceive of an idea as existing in some mind or other but no particular mind. And if this is so, he cannot allow that I can conceive of an idea as able to exist in a mind other than my own, for what I am here conceiving as possible is something that on his view is too indeterminate to be conceived.

It does not help in the least here that according to Berkeley many of our ideas exist in the mind of God as well as in our own mind; the ideas of sense are shared ideas, and since physical objects are public objects they may also be perceived by other people. We know that Berkeley wants to say this. The question is whether his own system leaves him room to do so. The fact that many of our ideas are shared with others does nothing to show how it is possible for us to conceive of them as existing in minds other than our own.

This conclusion is another reason, further to those considered at the end of chapter 5, why Berkeley cannot consistently adopt phenomenalism. For the phenomenalist approach is to say that it is sufficient for a collection of ideas to be a real thing if those ideas *could* exist in some mind or other, but no mind in particular. This sort of indeterminate relation to minds seems to me to be ruled out by the argument from abstraction.

If we cannot conceive of any idea other than our own, can we conceive of other minds than our own directly instead of via their contents? If not, each of us is committed to the strongest form of solipsism, which holds that there is no other possible owner of experiences than oneself. It would show that Berkeley cannot make the move he thinks so easy, when he says:

My own mind and my own ideas I have an immediate knowledge of; and by the help of these, do mediately apprehend the possibility of the existence of other spirits. (Third Dialogue, p. 232)

This would be the realisation of a danger to which we pointed earlier in this chapter, that the peculiarities of our method of finding out about ourselves affect the nature of the thing found out about. The method is unique, and its result emerges as unique too; the sort of thing which *this* method reveals to us is a thing of which there *couldn't* be a second example.

It is not easy, given Berkeley's approach, to make sense of there being a consciousness other than one's own. More is required for this than that one should simply repeat the words "there is another object which is like me but not me". We have to comprehend this possibility, not just allude to it uncomprehendingly. But any consciousness of which we can conceive seems to be our consciousness. We might hope to conceive of there being another window on the world than ourselves by imagining the way things look to others. But this won't do the trick. What we are imagining is not how things would look to others, but how they would look to us if our body were where that body is. In the case of pain, we are imagining what it would be like to feel a pain in that knee rather than in one of these. But the person we are imagining feeling the pain is still ourself.

Berkeley's position on the problem of other minds is a classic one. We start from a conception of ourself, and derive from it a conception of others like ourself. And the reply to it is classic too. It is that if we insist in this way on starting from our own case we will never be able to move out to establish even the possibility of others.

There is, I think, a vestige of a reply that Berkeley might make to all this. In discussing Berkeley's argument or arguments for the existence of God we suggested that in his view we experience the ideas of sense as independent of ourselves: independent of our will, that is. At this point the independence appeared as an experienceable feature of the ideas, in virtue of which when properly understood it emerged that we experienced these ideas *as* the ideas of a mind other than ourselves. This does not yet show that Berkeley is entitled to the claim that we can conceive of ideas which are not ours, if only because at this moment they are ours – and God's as well. But it might be a way of beginning to make sense of the idea that we can experience the otherness of another mind directly – its distinctness from ourselves. For one oddity of the suggestion that we experience the independence of our ideas of sense is that independence is a causal feature. But ideas, being passive, do not have causal features of this sort. This being so, the experience of independence must be experience of something that can have causal features, namely another mind: in this case, the mind of God. Other more normal minds could not, perhaps, be experienced in this way. But our route to the very conception of another mind may be preserved in this way by saying that we work through the experience of the will of God.

This manoeuvre is certainly one which would appeal to Berkeley. Later, in the *Alciphron*, he argues that our knowledge of the existence of others like ourselves is founded on less evidence than is our knowledge of the existence of God. Using the conception of the ideas of sense as utterances of God, he argues that it is largely the utterances of others that reveal to us the existence of other minds. But since the whole world around us is a series of God's utterances, when properly understood we have vastly more reason to believe that God exists than we have to believe that the bodies like ours are activated by minds like ours.

But this is speculation. The position as we have it without reliance on this dubious detour is that Berkeley is not able to make good sense of our ability to conceive of the possibility of minds other than ourselves. He is inmeshed in a solipsism of the most extreme form.

Is this sort of solipsism a tenable position? One classic reply to it is that the solipsist cannot even make sense of himself as a subject or owner of experience; for in losing the ability to conceive of the possibility of others like oneself one loses the ability to conceive of oneself. This is the conclusion of Wittgenstein's argument against the possibility of a private language, commonly called the Private Language argument.[3] Wittgenstein argues that the solipsist, having denied himself the luxury of supposing that there may be others like himself, still needs a language in which to think. But the solipsist has no means of learning a language. The only available method of getting a language going would be by concentrating on one's own sensations, and giving them names whose meaning is fixed by the sensations they are the names of. Thus one might focus on a particular sensation and say "This is pain", and hope that one had thereby given a meaning to the word 'pain'. But this attempt at ostensive definition will not and cannot work. This is not the place for a detailed account of Wittgenstein's reasons for this conclusion, but one of them is the claim that ostensive definition only makes sense if we already have a going language and cannot be used to construct a language from scratch. Suppose that I point at a chair and say "By 'chair' I mean *that*". Nothing in what I have done can succeed in creating the desired meaning for the word 'chair' unless I can say what it is about the object I am pointing to that I am taking as relevant. For example, I might say "that sort of furniture", and this would improve matters; but to do this I would of course need to know the meaning of 'furniture' already. Similarly with sensations, saying "By 'pain' I mean *that*" will only achieve the desired effect if I have some means of separating characteristics that are to be

---

[3] The argument is at §§ 243 ff. of his *Philosophical Investigations*; I attempt an exposition of it in ch. 5 of my *An Introduction to Contemporary Epistemology* (Oxford: Basil Blackwell 1985).

relevant from those that are not. Pains have plenty of characteristics that are not relevant to their being pains: duration, intensity, location, cause and ownership, to name a few. And only someone who knew that these things are to be excluded, i.e. who already has a language, could use an ostensive definition to give the word 'pain' the intended meaning in the way suggested.

This is only one of Wittgenstein's arguments in this area, but it is already enough to cast doubt on the hope that the solipsist is at least equipped to talk to himself, if not to others. If this is right, the solipsist's position is impossible. And this is the argument that if we cannot conceive of others, we cannot conceive of ourselves either; for we would have no language in which to express that conception.

This seems to show that within Berkeley's system the only available conception of oneself is as an ownerless system of floating ideas. This is the conclusion that Hume drew, but it really amounts to a complete rewriting of Berkeley's philosophy. Ideas would cease to be dependent objects, because there seems now to be no reason why individual ideas cannot exist in isolation from others. And this would remove the Berkeleian argument against phenomenalism mentioned a few paragraphs ago, for it would mean that there *can* be such things as ideas which someone may have but which no-one actually has. Such ideas are simply hanging around waiting for others to join them.

If Berkeley resists this rewriting, what chance has he of claiming that he knows his own existence as a thinking active being by what he calls 'reflection'? Is there really anything there to be reflected? Once we see the possibility that the self should turn out to be nothing but a system of floating ideas, appeal to reflection begins to seem empty. For if we were able by this reflection to generate a suitably substantial conception of ourself, surely there should be no real problem in generating the conception of another such, by simple reduplication. But there is such a problem, and this is sufficient to cast doubt on the claim that by a simple act of mind I can acquire a conception of myself as an independent active being, the separate owner of the ideas that are mine.

In this chapter we have seen a number of difficulties for Berkeley. His philosophy of mind seems to be beset with more and more severe difficulties than is his idealist account of the world of sense. Those that have emerged have concerned the nature of human action and our knowledge of ourselves and of others, which are really the central topics in the philosophy of mind. The sceptical may be forgiven the suspicion that this is why the second Part of the *Principles*, in which Berkeley intended to deal with these matters more fully, never saw the light of day. Berkeley himself, when questioned on this matter by the American philosopher Samuel Johnson, excused himself thus:

As to the Second Part of my treatise concerning the *Principles of Human Knowledge*, the fact is that I had made a considerable progress in it; but the manuscript was lost about fourteen years ago, during my travels in Italy, and I never had leisure since to do so disagreeable a thing as writing twice on the same subject. (Letter of November 25, 1729)

I can see no reason to cast doubt on this explanation other than a general mistrust of Berkeley's ingenuity, in which I cannot join.

10
Conclusion

It seems a pity, having got this far, to end our account of Berkeley on the note of glum resignation that may have crept into the last chapter. I prefer to conclude by stressing again what I take to be the enduring aspects of Berkeley's philosophy in the hope that the good things will stay in the mind when the less successful have been long forgotten. And I will end by contrasting the interpretation of Berkeley offered in this book with those offered elsewhere, so that readers may know which elements are more or less standard and agreed among contemporary commentators, and which are more contentious and therefore more worthy of suspicion. Up till now I have been more or less telling the story, and now I want to talk about the story I have told.

Central to any enthusiasm for Berkeley's philosophy must be some sympathy for his attack on the absolute conception of the world, in which we claim to conceive of the world as existing independent of and out of all relation to minds. The absolute conception sometimes offers itself as an answer to the question what the world would be like if there were no perceivers in it. If we take the notion of perception narrowly, referring only to sense perception, Berkeley's answer would be that it would not differ in any way from the rich world of sensory qualities with which we perceivers are familiar. For the world of sense would still exist in God's mind, and exist in just the form that it in fact presents to us. God, however, does not strictly speaking perceive the world of sense. God has no senses, since the senses are causal recipients, and God's ideas are never the effects of anything other than himself. The world of sense is the product not of God's senses but of his imagination. It is his free creation.

If we take the notion of perception more widely, as Berkeley himself normally did, so as to include any form of awareness of an idea, there is for Berkeley no answer to the question what an unperceived world is like. And it is not that there is an answer to this question which unfortunately we cannot grasp. We know that the question cannot be answered because it makes no sense.

Associated with Berkeley's attack on the possibility of an absolute conception of the world is his attack on the distinction between primary and secondary qualities. There are two sides to this association. The first is that the absolute conception is often itself associated with the primary/secondary distinction, since proponents of it commonly restrict themselves to the primary qualities and exclude the secondary ones from the world as absolutely conceived. This depends on the exact account given of the secondary qualities. If they are thought of as sensory properties, existing in the objects just as they seem to us to be, nothing like them is allowed by proponents of the absolute conception to be present in the world as absolutely conceived. If however they are thought of as dispositions or powers in the objects to cause certain sense experiences in us, there may still remain a chance that they should persist in the world as absolutely conceived. In the absolute conception there are no perceivers, but we might still say that if there had been any perceivers there, they would have had such and such sense experiences, and because of this subjunctive conditional allow that the objects there do retain secondary qualities as well as primary ones. They are still coloured because they are still disposed to cause certain sense experiences in perceivers if there were any – only there aren't any. They retain the power to cause those sense experiences even though there is nothing around for those powers to operate on.

The other way in which the absolute conception and the primary/ secondary distinction are associated is that Berkeley's reasons for rejecting one are the same as his reasons for rejecting the other. It will be remembered that two versions of the distinction emerged. The first was Locke's version, which worked by contrasting those properties in the objects which resemble our ideas of them and those which do not. Berkeley argued forcefully that this way of drawing the distinction made no sense, and I found his arguments here convincing. The second version held instead that the primary and the secondary qualities are related to experience in entirely different ways. As Evans put it, to grasp the primary properties one must master a set of interconnected principles which make up an elementary theory – of primitive mechanics – into which these properties fit, and which alone gives them sense. On the other hand, it is perfectly possible to distil the concept of colour out of certain sense experiences without any underlying theory at all, and indeed this may be the only way of acquiring that concept.

Berkeley would have rejected this more modern construct with the same vigour with which he rejected its classical antecedent. As we saw in chapter 6, he would have insisted that this way of drawing the distinction separates the primary qualities too far from our experiences of them. It makes them too theoretical. We may suggest in reply that Berkeley's own account makes them not theoretical enough. Berkeley wants to say that concepts of primary qualities are simply extracted from experience in the way in which he imagines the concepts of secondary qualities to be. A reasonable reply claims against this that if it were so, it is not obvious how the concepts so extracted could ever be combined into the sort of interconnected theory which we know to be possible. But the best attempt to cope with this point runs in Berkeley's favour, leaving the primary/secondary distinction still in need of a clear and persuasive formulation. The best way to move is surely to allow that the concepts of neither the primary nor the secondary qualities can be extracted in the simple way that Berkeley imagines. It is true that without the relevant sorts of experience we are going to find it hard to start off, but equally true that our concept of colour, just like our concepts of weight, temperature, solidity etc., can become more sophisticated and more sensitive to the demands of surrounding theory, without losing altogether its links with its sensory origin. As our knowledge of colour grows, we accept that an object's colour can change with changes in the light, for example, and we begin to learn ways to predict and understand these changes. In short, our growing knowledge of physical and optical theory cannot but alter for the better the concept of colour with which we started. In this respect the concept of colour is no different from our concepts of the traditional primary qualities.

It should be compatible with the spirit of this reassimilation of the primary qualities to the secondary ones to find still some differences between them. We do not have to say with Berkeley that there are no differences at all, but only that whatever differences there are will be more differences of degree than of kind. Of course there are things to be said about the differences between colour and shape, but these have been exaggerated by thinking of colour as a sensory quality and shape as a theoretical one. This immediately introduces a bleak contrast between sensation and theory, and with it an extreme version of the contrast between primary and secondary qualities. We should reject this extreme version and any variant of it, and seek rather to reconstruct an account under which such differences as there are between colour (e.g.) and shape (e.g.) are admitted without becoming the basis of a large metaphysical divide: that is, without grounding any version of the absolute conception.

The matter reminds me of attempts to persuade us that there is an enormous difference between moral properties such as goodness and badness and non-moral properties such as squareness and length (note that the contrast is with the primary qualities, as before). By concentrating on extreme cases, one is led to see rightly that there is a difference between them, and led wrongly to think that the difference cannot be a matter of degree, because the gap between the two extremes appears so large. A better approach, in my view, recognises a sort of spectrum on which goodness and badness are at one end and squareness etc. at the other, with the question what lies in the middle still unresolved. In a similar way, there should be room to admit the differences between colour and shape without this amounting to a distinction between the primary and the secondary on anything like the traditional lines.

With this caveat, it seems to me that Berkeley's general attack on the primary/secondary distinction is well founded, and that subsequent attempts to rewrite the distinction do not do much to mend matters.

It will be remembered that one of Berkeley's reasons for disliking the distinction was a sense that it led to a distortion of our experience. For it led us to feel that our experience of colour, for instance, somehow does not represent the world to us in quite the same way that our experience of shape and size does. This does not mean that we should distrust our sense of colour, exactly. That sense is still as reliable as ever, and likely to lead us astray only if we abuse it. It is rather that we can no longer feel that in respect of colour the world really is the sort of way it seems to us to be.

This is only one example of another worthwhile aspect of Berkeley's thought, namely his insistence on the need to write a philosophy which makes genuine sense of our experience. We must not distort that experience at the behest of our philosophy, for that is to destroy our only starting point. This is what one might elsewhere call a good realist intuition. It amounts to the presumption that the world is by and large the sort of way it seems to us to be, for any backsliding from this presumption leaves our experience in that respect a sort of conceptual oddity, from which we can only feel estranged. Berkeley's approach is always to strive to leave things as far as possible as they seem. One of his complaints against the so-called realists was just that they failed to do this. In one of his most purple passages, in the Second Dialogue, he extols the immensity and complexity of the universe, ending by asking:

Is not the whole system immense, beautiful, glorious beyond expression and beyond thought! What treatment then do those philosophers deserve, who would deprive these noble and delightful scenes of all reality? How should those principles be entertained, that lead us to think all the visible beauty of the creation a false imaginary glare? (p. 211)

In this sense Berkeley really felt that the realists were not as realistic about the world they claimed to experience as he was. First he held that they were not realist enough about the secondary qualities; this we have already seen. But another instance of the same charge concerns the independence of the world we sense. Berkeley wanted to agree that if we consider our experience aright we will, as the realists insist, be struck by the fact that we experience it as independent of us. And his idealism claims to give a satisfactory account of this independence. The world of sense is independent of us, since it is the creation of God, a selection of God's from among his own ideas. The realist account, however, fails in two directions. First, it gives an account of the independence of the world so extreme that it leaves the world beyond our grasp altogether. But, second, it only applies that account to half the properties we experience, namely the primary ones. Berkeley's own account attempts to walk the tightrope between these two failings, offering a genuine independence which is uniform for all experienced properties whatever. He offers a link between experience and independence, which the realists break.

This insistence on taking our experience seriously emerges clearly in Berkeley's argument for the existence of God. I argued in chapter 4 that even though he does not say that we experience the presence of God, nor that we experience God's power in providing the ideas of sense, still we cannot make the required sense of our experience of the world as spatial unless we accept the existence of a continuing mind permanently aware of every aspect of the perceived world. In the absence of such a mind our experience would make no sense, in Berkeley's view.

So, paradoxically, Berkeley's respect for realist intuitions emerges as a noteworthy aspect of his thought. And this is true also in the theory of perception, as we saw in chapter 6 where it appeared that Berkeley's account of perception offered the best way to understand the claims of the direct realist. However, since this matter hinges once again on the twin topics of independence and the reality of the secondary qualities I shall not further enlarge on it.

As final evidence for Berkeley's tendencies towards direct realism we might consider this passage from the Third Dialogue:

I am of a vulgar cast, simple enough to believe my senses, and leave things as I find them. To be plain, it is my opinion, that the real things are those very things I see and feel, and perceive by my senses. These I know ... It is likewise my opinion, that colours and other sensible qualities are on the objects. I cannot for my life help thinking that snow is white, and fire hot. (pp. 229–30)

The last point that I want to stress concerns the argument from abstraction. We decided in chapter 9 that this argument proves too much, and this naturally leads us to be suspicious of it on earlier appearances. But we are not yet justified in rejecting it entirely and reverting to our realist slumbers. First, we have as yet no idea what is really wrong with it; we only know that it needs amendment somewhere. Second, we cannot know in advance that the amendments will not leave the effectiveness of the argument against the realist conception of the independence of the world of sense unimpaired. Berkeley's arguments seem to create a genuine challenge to realism, and any difficulties for the challenge do little to rehabilitate the theory challenged.

Other interpretations

To start with the negative first, my general view that Berkeley's philosophy of mind is far less successful than is his philosophy of matter is a fairly widespread position. Whatever one's interpretation of the argument in the First Dialogue about conceiving an unconceived tree, one is likely to end up saying that it commits Berkeley to solipsism. This conclusion can, however, emerge in different ways, which it is important to distinguish. The wrong way is to see the argument about the unconceived tree in the First Dialogue as the claim that the proposition 'I conceive of an unconceived tree' expresses a straight contradiction. If one takes this line, one immediately notices that the proposition 'I conceive of a tree which I do not conceive' is as contradictory as the first was. And one then concludes that Berkeley is committed to saying that one cannot conceive that anything should exist other than the contents of one's own mind.[1] This common charge is a mistake, because it rests upon an unsympathetic account of the argument in the First Dialogue. I argued rather that Berkeley's thoughts there are really to be seen as an expression of his argument from abstraction, and then in chapter 9 that this argument leads him into difficulties when he turns to the problem of Other Minds. My conclusion is the same, therefore, but the route to it is rather different.

The most distinctive feature of the interpretation of Berkeley's thought offered here is its stress on the argument from abstraction. Other commentators, with the notable exception of Grayling, seem to leave this element entirely out of account. Urmson writes "What I find odd is the claim of Berkeley that the doctrine of abstract ideas was closely connected with the belief in matter. I can think of no place where Locke or any other philosopher made use of the doctrine of abstract ideas to defend the intelligibility of matter".[2] Bennett agrees; he writes "I align myself with those who have trouble finding the supposed link between the theory of abstract ideas and materialism".[3] Pitcher promises an

---

[1] See G. Pitcher *Berkeley* (London: Routledge and Kegan Paul 1977), pp. 112–3.
[2] J. O. Urmson *Berkeley* (Oxford: Oxford University Press 1982), p. 29.
[3] J. Bennett *Locke, Berkeley, Hume: Central Themes* (Oxford: Oxford University Press 1971), p. 45.

investigation of "the connection that Berkeley alleges to exist between the doctrine of abstract ideas and the anti-Berkeleyan opinion that is so 'strangely prevailing amongst men'", but in fact the investigation promised never mentions abstraction at all.[4] Obviously the account given in this book goes against the trend of these passages, in trying to show explicitly how Berkeley's attack on the notion of abstract general ideas could be central to an attack on realism. It remains to be seen how significant this difference between approaches is.

A second distinctive feature of the interpretation offered here is its stress on Berkeley's use of sceptical arguments of the strongest form, arguments about our ability to understand the propositions in question rather than about the justification of our belief that they are true or about our knowledge of their truth. This stress on understanding, together with the charge that illegitimate abstraction creates incomprehensibility, leads to an account of Berkeley which focuses on questions about what we can or cannot conceive, and on whether the realist conception of an independent world is in fact as readily available to us as is claimed. As a result I have talked a great deal about conception and the conceivable, and rather less about perception and the perceivable. This distances my account from more standard rivals, of which there may be said to be two.

The first of these holds that Berkeley starts from the claim that the immediate objects of our awareness are sensory properties possessed by occupants of the physical world. But sensory properties cannot exist unsensed. Hence the immediate objects of awareness are things which we cannot suppose able to exist unperceived.[5]

It might be argued in favour of this account of Berkeley that it makes the best sense of his slogan 'esse est percipi'; certainly it seems to make better sense of this than I can, for on my account it looks as if the slogan ought to have been 'esse est concipi'. But this distinction evaporates when we realise that Berkeley did not draw in our way the distinction between perception and conception. Certainly he did not hold that the only real things are those that are perceived by us; an object is real enough if by God's decree it is perceptible to us. And for this it is necessary that God should conceive it.

This seems to me to undermine any charge that my interpretation of Berkeley overstresses conception at the expense of perception. In other respects, however, I do not need or intend to say that this rival interpretation is entirely confused or wrong. There is no doubt that

---

[4] Pitcher *Berkeley*, p. 63; cf. pp. 112–15.
[5] See J. Foster 'Berkeley on the physical world', in J. Foster and H. Robinson (eds) *Essays on Berkeley: A Tercentennial Celebration* (Oxford: Clarendon Press 1985), at p. 85.

Berkeley does argue in the sort of way that it is concerned to highlight, particularly in the First Dialogue. The question is rather how this interpretation relates to my own.

Granted that the secondary qualities are sensory qualities, why should Berkeley hold that the primary qualities are sensory qualities as well? One possibility is the disentangling argument, which insists that the primary qualities cannot be separated from the secondary ones. So if the secondary ones cannot exist unsensed, neither can the primary ones. But I argued in chapters 2 and 3 that Berkeley's attack on the primary/secondary distinction stemmed mainly from his view that an idea can resemble nothing but another idea, and that the basis for this view was his rejection of the use of abstraction which he saw as endemic to realism. With this in hand, the possibility of an absolute conception vanished, and this was the basic reason why we cannot conceive of an object that is shaped existing out of all relation to a mind. For we have reached a point where we hold, not so much that shape is a sensory property, but rather that whether it is a sensory property or not it cannot exist unsensed. This means that the first rival interpretation is not incompatible with, but rather in my view presupposes, my own account.

The second interpretation of Berkeley starts from the thought that a property cannot be instantiated – there cannot be an instance of that property – unless there is an object which in this instance has the property. Properties need bearers – they need objects to belong to. Now the secondary qualities are agreed not to be genuine properties of material objects; they are thought of as more like properties of the minds that perceive them. The bearers of secondary qualities, then, are minds; minds are the things that have them and are coloured etc.. And the primary qualities cannot be separated from the secondary ones; so they too must belong to whatever objects are the possessors of the secondary ones, namely minds. So all properties are properties of minds, and so no properties can exist (i.e. be instantiated) in the absence of minds. And this is why the relation to a mind is essential to the existence of any sensible thing (property).[6]

Here again I do not want to say that this interpretation of Berkeley is completely wrong. A passage which is particularly congenial to it occurs very early in the *Principles*:

From what has been said, it follows, there is not any other substance than *spirit*, or that which perceives. But for the fuller proof of this point, let it be considered, the sensible qualities are colour, figure, motion, smell, taste, and such like, that

---

[6] See A. Hausman 'Adhering to inherence: a new look at the old steps in Berkeley's march to idealism', *Canadian Journal of Philosophy*, 1984, 14, pp. 421–42.

is, the ideas perceived by sense. Now for an idea to exist in an unperceiving thing, is a manifest contradiction; for to have an idea is all one as to perceive: that therefore wherein colour, figure, and the like qualities exist, must perceive them; hence it is clear there can be no unthinking substance or *substratum* of those ideas. (P. 7)

Nonetheless it seems to me that there are problems for this interpretation. The first is that it seems to suggest that Berkeley made the mistake of holding that since the secondary qualities do not belong to material objects, they must belong to minds; for they need to belong to something, and minds are the only things left. This seems to me a dubious argument (though its dubiousness does not guarantee that Berkeley did not use it); but whether it is dubious or not we have independent reasons for thinking that it cannot have been Berkeley's central point. For elsewhere he writes:

Fifthly, it may perhaps be objected, that if extension and figure exist only in the mind, it follows that the mind is extended and figured; since extension is a mode or attribute, which (to speak with the Schools) is predicated of the subject in which it exists. I answer, those qualities are in the mind only as they are perceived by it, that is, not by way of *mode* or *attribute*, but only by way of *idea*; and it no more follows, that the soul or mind is extended because extension exists in it alone, than it does that it is red or blue, because those colours are on all hands acknowledged to exist in it, and nowhere else. (P. 49)

Here Berkeley is saying explicitly that neither colours nor shapes need an owner in the traditional sense. So I reject the basic move in this second rival interpretation. It seems to me in fact to take as Berkeley's central point something which, so far as it is a Berkeleian thought at all, is on his own showing a mere consequence of the idealism which he takes himself already to have established by the time we get to *Principles* 7 (note the phrase "From what has been said, it follows . . .").

One consequence of the stress which my interpretation lays on the notion of abstraction is, as I argued, that Berkeley cannot be seen as any sort of covert phenomenalist. Indeed I held in chapter 5 that it is not merely that Berkeley was not in fact a phenomenalist. Rather phenomenalism is incompatible with his initial reason for adopting idealism. This is a departure from the usual view, which is that phenomenalism is a very close relative of idealism, and that anyone tempted by idealism but who cannot bring himself to go the whole way with Berkeley should retreat to phenomenalism.[7] My view was the reverse, since I saw idealism as fundamentally more consistent than its apparently more flexible rival.

[7] See Bennett *Locke, Berkeley, Hume*, ch. 6, and Pitcher *Berkeley*, p. 162.

My account of Berkeley's argument for the existence of God goes in conscious opposition to the standard account of which Bennett is the main proponent. The suggestion that for Berkeley considerations of continuity were inseparable from considerations of independence, and hence that the thrust of his argument is more unified and also broader than Bennett allows, is also to be found in Grayling.[8] But I think that I go further than Grayling does in my suspicion that for Berkeley God is not so much the product of an inference as a being whose existence is imposed on us in our every experience, if only we would open our own eyes to him. The closer God is to us, the more Berkeley would be pleased.

In similar vein, my stress on the importance of the few remarks in the *Principles* on the subject of God's language is unusual. Most commentators have little to say on Berkeley's philosophy of science, and less on his flirtation with the idea that natural events are utterances of God's. But I see this idea as part and parcel of Berkeley's general tendency to find for God the most important role possible, and it seems to me to link his philosophy of science much more fruitfully to his general idealist position, with God as always as the hinge. The account of scientific explanation as interpretative which I offer in chapter 8 will not be found elsewhere in the literature, and I must admit that it is more reconstructed than discovered in the text. But I cannot feel that this is a matter for regret if freely admitted, and I think that Berkeley would only have welcomed this expansion of his position. The fertility of Berkeley's ideas spreads; his inventiveness is catching, I suppose. Like all great philosophy, it is at once unsettling and stimulating, and the first task of any critic is to build up before turning to demolition. I confess to finding Berkeley's idealist vision a huge tour de force, and hope that I have managed to express some of the attraction it has for me in a contagious way.

[8] See A. C. Grayling *Berkeley: The Central Arguments* (London: Duckworth 1986), ch. 2.5–6 and ch. 3.4.

Further Reading

This is not intended as a complete list of relevant or even of recommendable readings, but only as an introductory selection as a supplement to the text.

Books

M. R. Ayers, introduction to his *George Berkeley: Philosophical Works* (London: Dent 1975).

J. Bennett *Locke, Berkeley, Hume: Central Themes* (Oxford: Oxford University Press 1971).

A. C. Grayling *Berkeley: The Central Arguments* (London: Duckworth 1986).

G. Pitcher *Berkeley* (London: Routledge and Kegan Paul 1977).

I. C. Tipton *Berkeley: The Philosophy of Immaterialism* (London: Methuen 1974).

J. O. Urmson *Berkeley* (Oxford: Oxford University Press 1982).

Collections of articles

J. Foster and H. Robinson (eds) *Essays on Berkeley* (Oxford: Oxford University Press 1985).

C. B. Martin and D. M. Armstrong *Locke and Berkeley* (London: Macmillan 1968).

C. Turbayne (ed.) *Berkeley: Critical and Interpretative Essays* (Minneapolis: University of Minnesota Press 1982).

Suggested supplementary readings

Chapter 1

J. Locke *An Essay Concerning Human Understanding* (first published 1690), edited by John Yolton (London: Dent, Everyman's Library 1961), bk. 2, chs. 8–9.

P. Alexander 'Locke and Boyle on primary and secondary qualities', *Ratio*, 16, 1974, pp. 51–67; reprinted in I. Tipton (ed.) *Locke on Human Understanding* (Oxford: Oxford University Press 1977).

J. L. Mackie *Problems from Locke* (Oxford: Oxford University Press 1976) ch. 1.

Chapter 2

M. A. E. Dummett *Truth and Other Enigmas* (Oxford: Oxford University Press 1978), ch. 10 [on realism].

A. Gallois 'Berkeley's master argument', *Philosophical Review*, 1974, 83, pp. 55–69.

C. McGinn *The Subjective View* (Oxford: Oxford University Press 1983), pp. 80–90.

C. Peacocke 'Imagination, experience and possibility', in Foster and Robinson (eds) *Essays on Berkeley* [this article is not for beginners].

B. Williams *Descartes: the Project of Pure Enquiry* (Harmondsworth: Penguin Books 1978) pp. 64–7 and 244–9 [on the absolute conception].

B. Williams 'Imagination and the Self', *Proceedings of the British Academy*, 1966, 52, pp. 105–24; reprinted in P. F. Strawson (ed.) *Studies in the Philosophy of Thought and Action* (Oxford: Oxford University Press 1968) and in Williams' *Problems of the Self* (Cambridge: Cambridge University Press 1973).

Chapter 3

A. C. Grayling *Berkeley*, pp. 29–42, 89–92.

J. L. Mackie *Problems from Locke*, ch. 4.

G. Pitcher *Berkeley*, ch. 5.

Chapter 4

J. Bennett *Locke, Berkeley, Hume*, ch. 7.

A. C. Grayling *Berkeley*, ch. 2.5–6 and ch. 3.4.

Chapter 5

J. Bennett *Locke, Berkeley, Hume*, ch. 6.

A. C. Grayling *Berkeley*, ch. 2.4.

G. Pitcher *Berkeley*, ch. 10.

Chapter 6

J. Dancy *An Introduction to Contemporary Epistemology* (Oxford: Basil Blackwell 1985), ch. 1 [on sceptical arguments] and ch. 10 [on theories of perception].

G. Evans 'Things without the mind', in Z. van Straaten (ed.) *Philosophical Subjects: Essays Presented to P. F. Strawson* (Oxford: Clarendon Press 1980) esp. pt. 3.

C. McGinn *The Subjective View*, ch. 8.

Chapter 7

C. G. Hempel 'The function of general laws in history', *Journal of Philosophy*, 1942, 39, pp. 35–48; reprinted in H. Feigl and W. Sellars (eds) *Readings in Philosophical Analysis* (New York: Appleton-Century-Crofts 1949), pp. 459–71.

Chapter 8

H.P. Grice 'Meaning', *Philosophical Review*, 1957, 66, pp. 377–88; reprinted in P. F. Strawson (ed.) *Philosophical Logic* (Oxford: Oxford University Press 1967).

C. Taylor *Hegel* (Cambridge: Cambridge University Press 1975), pt. 1.

Chapter 9

D. Hume *A Treatise Concerning Human Nature* (first published 1748), edited by L. A. Selby-Bigge, revised by P. Nidditch (Oxford: Clarendon Press 1978), bk. 1, pt. 4, sec. 6.

N. Malcolm 'Knowledge of other minds', *Journal of Philosophy*, 1958, 55, pp. 969–78 [expounds Wittgenstein's arguments].

C. C. W. Taylor 'Action and inaction in Berkeley', in Foster and Robinson (eds) *Essays on Berkeley*.

L. Wittgenstein *Philosophical Investigations* (Oxford: Basil Blackwell 1953) §§ 243 ff.

Index